LET GO OF WORRY, EMBARRASSMENT AND REGRET

3 Steps To Happiness

JENNIFER ALISON

© 2015

Copyright © 2015 by Jennifer Alison Publishing

All rights reserved.
No part of this publication may be reproduced, distributed, or transmitted in any form or by any means, including photocopying, recording, or other electronic or mechanical methods, without the prior written permission of the publisher, except in the case of brief quotations embodied in critical reviews and certain other noncommercial uses permitted by copyright law.

"We all make mistakes, have struggles, and even regret things in our past. But you are not your mistakes, you are not your struggles, and you are here NOW with the power to shape your day and your future."

Steve Maraboli

About The Author

Dr. Jennifer Alison is a worldwide recognized author and speaker.

Dr Alison specializes in the treatment of anxiety disorders and related physiological issues and has published several papers as well as speaking at conferences around the world. Several years ago she turned her research and studies into books, aimed at giving the general public easily digestible information and practical advice, cutting out all the unnecessary and unhelpful surplus nonsense which fills many other publications. All of her books have gone on to be international best sellers.

Jennifer Alison divides her time between New York and London with her husband Stephen.

jenniferalisonauthor.com

Subscribe to the Dr. Jennifer Alison mailing list for news of new releases, free eBooks and exclusive extra content.

Sign up by clicking here and receive a FREE book of tips to deal with anxiety fast: http://eepurl.com/bwU1Rv

Table Of Contents

Introduction: Get Started On Changing Your Life!

Part One: Understanding Worry and How To Defeat It

The Worries People Face and The First Step To Eradicate Them

Why Are You Worried? Easily and Quickly Identify

Body, Mind and Behaviour

Why Excessive Worry is Dangerous

Dealing With Worries In Your Life Today

The Pointlessness Of Worrying: The Lightbulb Moment!

Worrying or Positive Thinking? You Decide!

A Recap On The Follies Of Worry

Let Go Of Worry and Restart Your Life Today!

Step One: Those Underlying Thoughts

Step Two: Know When To Let Go and Become Happy

4 Times In Life You Must Let Go!

Step Three: Treat Your Worry Like A To Do List

Your Worry To Do List: Taking Action Today!

Step Four: Stop Worry In Its Tracks

5 Steps To Freeing Yourself From Worry Immediately

The 5 Step Model To Letting Go Of Worry & Anxiety

Part Two: Embarrassment & Shame. The Hidden Curses

Dealing With The Embarrassment People Feel

Embarrassment and Guilt

Addressing Guilty Feelings

Eradicate The Guilt!

Embarrassment and Shame: Overcome and Progress

Realign Shameful Feelings

Embarrassment and Pride

Letting Go Of Embarrassment: Live A Happy Life!

Step One: The Underlying Belief

4 Common Experiences That Exaggerate Embarrassment

Step Two: Be Graceful About It and Keep It In Perspective

5 Fundamental Truths About Embarrassment

Step Three: Turn It Into Something Positive, Fast!

3 Ways To Make Your Embarrassment Positive

8 Proven Ways To Overcome Embarrassment

Part Three: Regrets & How To Move On

How The World Around Us Feeds Regret & How To Stop It!

Romantic Regrets

The Most Important Top Ten List You Will Ever Read: Deathbed Regrets

The Negative Effects Of Regret & How To Stop Them

Unhelpful Rumination

Letting Go Of Regret: Live Your Life!

Step One: Identify The What and Why

Step Two: Stop The Blame Game!

Step Three: Letting Go Of "Coulda, Woulda, Shoulda"

Step Four: Turn Your Regret Into Something Positive!

Step Five: Live In The NOW!

Step Six: Getting To Grips With Romantic Regret

6 Steps To A Positive Life

Recommended Books & Resources

Introduction: Get started on changing your life!

Worry, embarrassment, and regret can have a toxic effect on your self esteem, your moods, your relationships, your general outlook on life, and your true potential. Though these experiences are natural and may offer some positive insight from time to time, by nature they are unhelpful and often harmful. A life full of worry, embarrassment, and regret is usually one which is overly challenging and often disheartening. Feeling too much of these self conscious emotions can quickly lead to poor self image, hopelessness, a series of difficult relationships, and depression.

The negative feelings attached to worry, embarrassment, and regret can easily be turned into weapons you can use to beat yourself up with. They can be anchors holding you back from self progression and ultimately a happy and fulfilled life. They can become habitual toxic self beliefs that lead you to harmful thinking and harsh critiquing of yourself. This might lead to self limiting and self sabotaging behaviours that leave you isolated and deeply unhappy. It does not have to be this way.

By freeing yourself from the vice like grips of worry, embarrassment, and regret, your life will be infinitely happier and more successful. Learning to let go of future worries and stamp out past regrets will mean you can enjoy a lighter and more promising present. This is the goal of this text! This book will show you how to cut ties with your negative thoughts and harmful self evaluations so that you can realise your true potential and have a life of fulfilling experiences and healthy relationships.

This book is written in three parts: one for worry, one for embarrassment, and one for regret. The feelings you may be feeling in each of the three parts may at first not be completely obvious but over time they will become clear. Each part of this book begins by exploring the true nature of these feelings and then focuses on giving you the skills you need to eliminate them from your life and most importantly how to stop them from returning once the "honeymoon period" is over.

Living a life full of harmful emotions is like being trapped in a prison cell. There is a system of bars and locks holding you inside. In order to break free, you will first need to understand how the bars and locks work, then you will need the necessary tools to pick the locks. This is not a lengthy boo but also it is not a quick read. Nothing as profound as turning your life from unhappy to happy comes easy and without work – any book that tells you it does it frankly a scam. I am not here to trick you. I am here to help you but it will require you making effort too. But what is better? A few weeks of effort or a lifetime of unhappiness?

By focusing on both the knowledge you need to understand your negative feelings and the skills you need to break free of them, this book will give you everything you need to break free of that cell.

In no time at all, you will know what it's like to be free to love yourself and your life.

"Even though you may want to move forward in your life, you may have one foot on the brakes. In order to be free, we must learn how to let go. Release the hurt. Release the fear. Refuse to entertain your old pain. The energy it takes to hang onto the past is holding you back from a new life. What is it you would let go of today?"

Mary Manin Morrissey

Part One: Understanding Worry and How To Defeat It!

"If you ask what is the single most important key to longevity, I would have to say it is avoiding worry, stress and tension. And if you didn't ask me, I'd still have to say it."
George Burns

The word "worry" comes from the Greek "merimnao" which means "to divide the mind". When someone is deliberating between ways of approaching a problem, they might be said to be "in two minds". Decision making is a big part of life and entirely unavoidable. You are forced to make countless decisions each day, from what to wear in the morning, to what to eat for lunch, to what school is best for your children. Every problem you face comes with its own options, its own gravity, and its own potential outcomes. Each decision you make comes with its own consequence, both positive and negative. This means some decisions are easier to make than others.

For instance, the consequence of choosing to have one more glass of wine generally won't take up too much of your intellectual energy whereas choosing to change to your career path might take some lengthy deliberation. In this light you can see that worrying is a very natural and necessary process when it comes to decision making. But what happens when your worry becomes more than a just a tool for decision making and begins to negatively effect all areas of your life?

"Worry does not empty tomorrow of its sorrow, it empties today of its strength."
Corrie ten Boom

If you imagine your mind or your thoughts as being "divided" constantly, you might better understand what is going on when you are worrying. As you wrestle with opposing feelings, deliberate over pros and cons, and struggle to come to conclusions, your mind becomes agitated, exhausted, and you may struggle to stay focused. When you are worrying in extreme or chronic ways, you are subjected to a "divided mind" for prolonged periods of time. It's hard to imagine how anyone could come to a productive conclusion when living in a constant state of worry, let alone achieve any sense of peace of mind. An unhealthy and unhappy way to live!

Everyone experiences worry from time to time, this is perfectly natural. I doubt anyone could honestly claim otherwise and if they do, best not to trust them! When worrying is used for constructive thinking and problem solving, it can be quite beneficial. It may spark some smart thinking about how to cope with a variety of situations and circumstances. However, when worry gets the better of you if can become a near constant negative force which can be detrimental to all parts of your life. Worry that becomes all-consuming could hold you back from reaching any conclusions at all. It could end up stopping you from progressing in all walks of life. It could have detrimental effects on your mood, your relationships with others, and your overall happiness.

The problem with worry is that it is based in thoughts about the future; a thing you cannot predict or control. For this reason, excessive worrying has no true purpose, but it does have very real effects. Can you imagine a time in your life when you worried excessively about something and worrying actually changed the outcome of the situation? Chances are, you can't. You may have worried about something to a reasonable degree and identified some action you could take to solve a problem. But with excessive worry, positive results are few and far between. Now think of a time you worried excessively about something and it had a negative effect on you or others around you. I'd bet there are plenty of examples of this. I can certainly think of plenty from my own past.

Think about times you worried so much you lost sleep, became ill, had an argument, failed to enjoy a night out or special occasion, or worried so much you became unfocused and forgetful. Think about times you were so worked up with worry that you avoided something rather than taking a risk such as applying for a promotion or offering your opinion in a meeting or family discussion.

Excessive worrying is harmful and pointless. It will not change the future, no matter how much that little voice in your head tells you it will. The only thing excessive worrying does is cause you restlessness and tension. Being able to recognise the harmful effect your worry has on you is the first step toward letting go of it.

The Worries People Face and The First Step To Eradicating Them!

Studies have shown that triggers of worry vary depending on age, gender, marital status, social status, and cultural background. While research shows that young people and students tend to focus their worry on relationships, financial issues, work, their future, and their self confidence, older people tend to worry more about health concerns and the happiness of others.

Interestingly, the prevalence of worry on the whole, actually reduces significantly with age with the height of worrying effecting people in their twenties and thirties. Surveys show that the majority of worrying is done at home (more specifically in the bedroom) between the hours of 9pm and 3am. This statistic helps shed some light on how much of a disturbance worry can be to your sleep cycle and your close relationships. It's no wonder people who worry excessively are often fatigued and therefore irritable or lack focus at various points throughout the day

When worry ceases to function as a constructive problem solving device and becomes instead, a near constant obsession of life's uncertainties, it begins to cause problems. Small problems at first which can quickly lead to big problems if not properly dealt with. People experiencing worry like this may be diagnosed as having Generalised Anxiety Disorder (GAD). GAD is, as you can imagine, a constant state of intense worry focused on just about anything regardless of its actual brevity or potential impact on their lives. Though people suffering from GAD worry about very similar things to people without it, their worry is distinguished by its perceived uncontrollable nature and its intensity.

Inevitably, everyone will worry at certain times in their lives; however, it is important to recognise when your worry is becoming bigger than you. You need to know when it is taking over your life. Use the following exercise to get to know the nature of your worry, recognise its commanding presence in your life and see how your behaviour may be adding to your worry. This exercise should help you begin to gain perspective.

Why Are You Worried? Easily and Quickly Identify!

"Learn from yesterday, live for today, hope for tomorrow. The important thing is not to stop questioning"
Albert Einstein

Write a list of 5 things that are worrying you. These could be things that are troubling you right now or things that seem to always trouble you.

Think deeply about why these things are causing you so much worry and write down a few reasons for each of your worries. Take your time on this. Do not just write down what you *think* you should be worried about. Be honest with yourself (nobody else needs to see this remember!) and write your worries as open and truthfully as you can.

Next, make a note of any behaviours you might be exhibiting that could be exaggerating each of your worries such as:

1 - Always feeling the need to do better or be the best at things to the point it makes you sad or angry if you are not.

2 - Leading an overly stressful lifestyle by taking on too many projects at once or insisting on doing everything yourself, constantly refusing the help of others.

3 - Placing too much importance on things that are insignificant (giving the same amount of worry to picking up the dry cleaning as you do to paying your mortgage, without any sense of balance).

4 - Feeling overly responsible for things that are happening around you or to people you know. Having little or no sense that other people are responsible for their own actions and decisions.

5 - Always putting yourself in charge or taking the blame when things go wrong.

6 - Comparing yourself to other people, without a sense of balance or realism.

7 - Always expecting the worst outcome, often for no particular reason.

8 - Focusing on what others will think of you if you fail, constantly worried about being judged negatively.

Finished? Are you certain? Have you been honest? Have you been open?

Finally, for each of your worries ask yourself if worrying is helping the future outcome of your problems or causing you extra stress. Be honest with yourself. I realize I am repeating the *"be honest with yourself"* thing but this is only because it is absolutely vital in order to deal with these issues.

"Being entirely honest with oneself is a good exercise"
Sigmund Freud

Body, Mind, And Behaviour

"Food for the body is not enough. There must be food for the soul."
Dorothy Day

When you worry, your body reacts the same way it would if you were in physical danger. Stress hormones such as adrenaline and cortisol flow through your bloodstream equipping your body for action. You may experience physical symptoms such as sweating or increased heart rate. This is your body's instinctive response to danger, often called the "fight or flight" response.

The fight-or-flight response, also known as the acute stress response, refers to a physiological reaction that occurs in the presence of something that is terrifying, either mentally or physically.
You can probably think of a time when you experienced the fight-or-flight response. In the face of something frightening, your heartbeat quickened, you began breathing faster, and your entire body became tense and ready to spring into action. This response can happen in the face of an imminent physical danger (such as encountering a growling dog during your morning jog) or as a result of a more psychological threat (such as preparing to give a big presentation at school or work).

By priming your body for action, you are better prepared to perform under pressure. The stress created by the situation can actually be helpful, making it more likely that you will cope effectively with the threat. This type of stress can help you perform better in situations where you are under pressure to do well, such as at work or school. In cases where the threat is actually life threatening, the fight-or-flight response can actually play a critical role in your survival. By gearing you up to fight or flee, the fight-or-flight response makes it more likely that you will survive the danger.

The *problem* with "fight or flight" is that it is there to protect you from predators, not from things like difficult relationships, financial concerns, or work stress! Having these stress hormones coursing through your body for a prolonged period of time is **proven** to have detrimental effects on your blood pressure, cholesterol levels, nervous system, glands, and heart and may increase your risk of stroke, stomach ulcers, and even heart attacks.

In addition to those more long term effects, you may be experiencing a number of short term physical concerns such as headaches, back pain, upset stomach, and muscle tension. Your immune system may be affected leaving you more susceptible to everything from colds and flus to much more serious illnesses. The more you worry and the more depleted your immune system becomes, the more you may experience exhaustion and fatigue. You may develop skin rashes or find conditions such as asthma and migraine are aggravated.

"Do not anticipate trouble, or worry about what may never happen. Keep in the sunlight."
Benjamin Franklin

Not only does excessive worrying have a negative effect on your body, it also affects your brain, your mood, and your behaviour. Constant worrying makes it hard to focus on tasks and can cause insomnia. You may experience a loss of libido due to your worry or you may become forgetful and absent minded. You may have trouble eating or you may start overeating. Excessive worry is often directly linked to weight problems. You may even become neglectful of your own health requirements such as taking medication on time or recognising when you need to take a break. Excessive worrying may lead to paranoia, depression, or catastrophic beliefs about your own future. You may wind up becoming withdrawn and have problems connecting with others and maintaining relationships as a result of your constant worry.

Below is a list illustrating some ways excessive worry may be affecting your body, mind, and behaviour negatively.

Why Excessive Worry is Dangerous

- Your Body

- Headaches
- Muscle tension or pain
- Chest pain
- Fatigue
- Change in sex drive
- Stomach upset
- Sleep problems
- Hair loss
- Regular periods of illness
- Blurred vision
- Trembling
- Restlessness

- Your Mind
- Anxiety
- Lack of motivation or focus
- Irritability or anger
- Sadness or depression
- Negative outlook on life
- Lowered self esteem
- Fearfulness
- Inability to problem solve
- Inability to plan ahead
- Resentment toward others
- Malaise

- Your Behaviour
- Overeating or under eating
- Angry outbursts
- Drug or alcohol abuse
- Excessive cigarette smoking
- Social withdrawal
- Avoidance of any activity or thought that may worry you
- Spontaneous unplanned actions like quitting a job or ending a relationship
- Self harm
- Use of aggressive language or physical violence

- Passive behaviour
- Lack of interest in work or recreation
- Placing restrictions on yourself or your future
- Having trouble maintaining relationships
-

"Worry is interest paid on trouble before it comes due."
Walter Ralph Inge

Dealing With Worries In Your Life Today

Look again at the list from the previous section and take note of how many of these effects are present in your life due to constant worrying. Write them down. Be honest with yourself.

Each item on your list is contributing factor to your overall outlook on life. Each item on your list could be holding you back from your true potential and full happiness.

Look at each item on your list one at a time and think about ways your life could be better without them. Write them down. For example: If you are suffering from fatigue, life without it might be "well rested" or "energetic". If you are avoiding taking risks with your career, life without that avoidance could mean "a brighter future" or "increased excitement".

Now look at all the positive ways your life could benefit from letting go of worry. Meditate on thoughts of release and inner peace. Do not worry too much about *how* you are going to let go of the worries, just relax and think about how different your life would be without them. Picture it. How it looks, how it sounds, how it feels.

The Pointlessness Of Worrying: The Lightbulb Moment!

"If you have a problem that can be fixed, then there is no use in worrying.
If you have a problem that cannot be fixed, then there is no use in worrying."
Buddhist Proverb

I doubt that anyone would argue with the idea that worrying cannot and will not change the future. This means that excessive worrying serves no purpose. Rather, as you have already learned, it is damaging to your outlook on life, your relationships, your potential, and your overall physical and psychological wellbeing. No one can predict the future. No one can shape the outcome of all of life's Unknowns. No matter how many times you imagine the future, you cannot predict it. Therefore, focusing all your energy on the future is a <u>waste of time</u>!

What's more is that when you're worrying, you are usually imagining the worst case scenario. You may think that you are "preparing yourself for the worst" but in essence what you are doing is building a belief that nothing will ever turn out the way you want it to. You are convincing yourself that everything will turn out badly all the time which is pessimistic and most likely untrue. Think of how draining repetitive negative thoughts like this can be to your mood and your outlook on life. Think of how morose your life would seem if you had no hope. Think of how sour you would come to feel under the weight of all that negativity day in and day out! Think of what it's like to be around someone who is endlessly imagining a dark and dreary future. It is tedious and torturous. Lonely and hopeless. And above all, **<u>it is pointless!</u>**

"It aint no use putting up your umbrella till it rains."
Alice Caldwell Rice

When you are consumed with worry, you can lose your will to make changes for the better. If you believe that everything will turn out badly, you will naturally want to give up. This might mean you continue to let life happen to you rather than actually living it. You just "muddle through", you go through the motions of life but you're not really going anywhere because you are being held back by this unproductive, all-consuming worry. Think of the amount of time you spend worrying and imagine what you could do with that time. You could educate yourself, create something outstanding, make a difference in the world, enjoy your life! Instead, excessive worrying keeps you right where you are, anchored to the same spot, day after day, year after year. Not a pleasant thought, right?

"As a rule, men worry more about what they can't see than about what they can."
Julius Caesar

Worrying is no more than simply being afraid. If you are constantly afraid, you will never do anything in life. You will always have an excuse to avoid experiencing new things. You will continuously shy away from taking risks. You will let opportunities pass you by again and again. How could you be happy living in this way?

You only get one life to live. Spending it in fear shouldn't be an option. In order to live the life you deserve, you must learn to let go of worry. The following section will help you to identify how excessive worrying is limiting your life and how to start dealing with it!

Worrying or Positive Thinking? You Decide!

"If you believe that feeling bad or worrying long enough will change a past or future event, then you residing on another planet with a different reality system."
William James

People who worry excessively often miss opportunities in life due to avoidance and fear.
Think about some ways your experience of excessive worrying is holding you back in life.

Think about your career:
Are you happy with it?
Would you prefer to be doing something different?
Have you avoided taking risks during the course of your career so far?

Think about your relationships:
Are you shying away from having meaningful relationships with others due to fear of failure?
Do you avoid relationships because you worry about your potential effect on others?
Do you hear yourself regularly making excuses about why your relationships are they way they are?
Have you run away from love or affection?

Think about yourself in relation to your hopes and dreams:
Are you where you want to be in life?
Have you compromised your hopes and dreams due to worry or fear?
Have you resisted the urge to follow your dreams because you're worried you might fail?

Next, think about any times you have expected the worst to happen but things actually ended in a positive way and write these things down.

Ask yourself:
Did worrying affect you? How?
Did worrying affect the outcome of the situation?
Do you believe your worrying was time well spent?

Finally, reflect on how much time you spend worrying about the future versus how much time you spend living in the here and now. Look back over the limitations in your life that are caused by worry. Look over the things you have shied away from out of fear.

Ask yourself why.

This is a very important section. Do not breeze over this. Take the time. Go for a walk or a long drive and really think about your answers. A lightbulb starting to go off in your head?

"Worry affects the circulation, the heart, the glands, the whole nervous system. I have never known a man who died from over work, but many who died from doubt."
Charles Horace Mayo

A Recap On The Follies Of Worry

The next part of this book will focus on how you can free yourself from worry for good, but for now, let's recap what you've learned so far.

1.) Worrying is natural and when used correctly it can be a helpful tool in problem solving; however, when worry is excessive, it can easily get the better of you and become a source of great negativity in your life.

2.) Worrying may be exaggerated by tendencies such as perfectionism, leading an overly stressful life, placing too much importance on insignificant things, or feeling responsible for too many things.

3.) Excessive worrying can have detrimental effects on your physical health, your overall mood, and your behaviour. As such, it may isolate you from others and hold you back from self-progression.

4.) Worrying is pointless as it is based in a future you cannot predict or change. Worrying makes you afraid of the future and may cause you to miss opportunities and lead a sorrowful or limited life.

"No man ever sank under the burden of the day. It is when tomorrows burden is added to the burden of today, that the wright is more than a man can bear."
George Macdonald

Let Go Of Worry and Restart Your Life Today!

"When I look back on all the worries, I remember the story of the old man who said on his deathbed that he had a lot of trouble in his life, most of which never happened."
Winston Churchill

You now know that worrying is pointless, damaging, and a waste of your time. You know that it is holding you back from taking risks and trying new things. You know that worry is keeping you anchored to the spot, unable to reach your goals. You may feel that worry is causing you unnecessary stress, depression, or overall discontentment. Now it's time to let go of it for good and to restart your life! Today! This section will show you how to free yourself from worry in just four simple steps.

Step One: Those Underlying Thoughts!

When letting go of worry, the first thing you will need to do figure out what harmful thoughts or beliefs are hidden beneath it. Think of this as getting to the root of the problem. No matter what worries are bubbling at the surface, there is always something bigger deep down keeping it alive. This could be many little things or one big thing, but no matter what it is, it will probably take some self exploration to discover it.

When you are in a safe and settled mindset, take some time to think about any underlying thoughts that might be lurking in your worries. If you find it difficult to concentrate on your thoughts, write them down, talk to a friend, or use a recording device as a private audience. You should engage in this activity regularly and always when you are feeling relaxed. Self discovery can be very difficult if you are in a heightened state of emotion.

To help you along with this process and to get your started, here are a few common self beliefs underlying excessive worrying.

5 Common Underlying Thoughts Of Chronic Worriers

1.) Happiness is something you must earn or buy.

There are a number of outdated beliefs about earning happiness. That is to say, you have to work hard to achieve happiness or you must go through a certain amount of pain and suffering before you are due any real happiness. These beliefs are not only untrue, but they can act as lifelong barriers to any feelings of happiness or contentment.

Furthermore, beliefs that money will ensure happiness are more common than you may think. Even if you don't often think consciously about money or dwell on it, the media and the world around you could be getting into your subconscious beliefs. Advertisements about what you need to be happy are everywhere and the world around you can be competitive to damaging degrees. These influences are telling you that you must have a fancy car, great skin, or a designer kitchen to be happy. They are telling you that if you don't have all the expensive things your siblings or neighbors have, you are not successful nor deserving of happiness.

Thoughts like these can settle like a puddle in the back of your mind. They might entice you to you over work and over spend; both of which will only increase your worry and anxiety.

2.) Worrying is helping me.

There is a part of you that may believe your worrying is serving a purpose. Deep down you may think that worrying is productive, that it's helping you prepare for the future or cope with a loss. This could lead to you becoming attached to your worry; holding on to it like a security blanket.

If you identify an underlying belief like this you must remind yourself again and again that worrying is NOT helping you. Rather, it is causing your fight or flight response to kick in unnecessarily putting you in a physically heightened state which will only result in tension and exhaustion. Challenge your underlying belief by reminding yourself that worrying is not only pointless, it also acts as an obstacle to clear thinking. The more you worry, the less you will be able to tackle life's obstacles and challenges.

Do not underestimate the power of self-talk. If you want to be able to let go of worry and anxiety, you will have to gain control of your thoughts. Keep practicing self-talk to rationalize and slow your thinking down.

3.) I am scared of the unknown.

One of the hardest things to cope with in life is unpredictability. If we knew what lay in our future at all times we could prepare for it better and control how things turn out. This desire to paint your own future is natural and common; however, it may lead to crippling a fear of the unknown.

In life, you will experience negative and painful experiences. Accepting that illness, loss, and death are a part of life is key in letting go of future fear. There are many things you will not be able to control in the course of your life and worrying will not prevent them from happening. Rather, worrying might cause you to miss the happy, exciting, and fulfilling parts of life. Challenge yourself to allow space in your mind for the unknown.

4.) I am not good enough.

Negative beliefs about yourself could be causing you exaggerated levels of worry and anxiety. Deep-rooted negative thoughts are often hidden far beneath the surface of your conscious mind. These may be things that someone once said to you that you've never let go of. They might be the result of an overly critical parent or a highly competitive sibling.

Negative beliefs about yourself might not be as obvious as "I'm not smart enough" or "I'm not worth it"; rather, they are often much more subtle such as "I've never really achieved that much" or "I'll never have as much as so-and-so". Similarly, if you are in the habit of focusing on what you don't have, you may be subtly adding to negative self-beliefs. The more you tell yourself that you are "different", "less successful", or experiencing "less opportunity" than other people, the more you are telling yourself that you are not good enough and you are not worthy of happiness or easiness in life.

"Once you replace negative thoughts with positive ones, you'll start having positive results"
Willie Nelson

Self-acceptance is hard for many people. Self-love is even harder. If you identify as someone suffering with deep-rooted self-doubt, remind yourself regularly to judge yourself based on your accomplishments, not other people's. Your life is yours. It has presented its own unique obstacles and opportunities. You have made good choices and bad. You've experienced triumphs and failures. Remind yourself regularly of things you have overcome. Resist the urge to compare yourself to others. They live their life, you live yours.

5.) Other people are happy all the time.

"When you are content to be simply yourself and don't compare or compete, everybody will respect you."
Lao Tzu

There is a very common misconception about the lives of others. When you see people, you are seeing themselves as they want to be perceived by others. You see them in their best outfits, at the best times in their marriage, smiling and laughing, well organized and content. It can be hard to resist believing that other people's lives are perfect. Therefore, by focusing on the happiness of others, you can end up in a state of self pity and useless competition.

It is important to remember that every person experiences difficulties and no one's life is perfect. More importantly, it is vital to let go of a belief in an all-encompassing happiness. Discontentment, disappointment, and dissatisfaction are a part of life. If you are constantly striving for an all-encompassing happiness you will only focus on that which is wrong in your life. This could lead to endless stress and worry about things you feel you must achieve. Much like trying to find the end of a rainbow, seeking this naive idea of "Happiness" could lead you on a fruitless and tiring trek.

Remind yourself often to recognise the things you already have which make you happy. Remind yourself of your achievements thus far. Let yourself enjoy the happiness you have in the here and now rather than focusing on the happiness you want in your future.

"I vow to let go of all worries and anxiety in order to be light and free"
Thich Nhat Hanh

Step Two: Know When To Let Go And Become Happy!

"Yesterday is not ours to recover, but tomorrow is ours to win or lose."
Lyndon B. Johnson

One of biggest contributing factors of excessive worrying is a desire to control things that you cannot. Letting go of worry can be so challenging that it leads to incessant rumination and feelings of deep unhappiness. It is a vicious circle which can be difficult to get out of. Difficult but by no means impossible! This is why knowing when to let go is so important to freeing yourself from excessive worry. The following steps will help you learn to recognise when enough is enough!

4 Times In Life You Must Let Go!

1.) When the ball isn't in your court.

One of the things that plagues worriers more than anything is other people. You may be worried about a decision that your boss will make that could shape your future. You might be worried about how your friends will feel about a choice you've made. You might be worried about how your partner will react to something that is important to you.

You must remember that not matter what you do, you cannot change another person's feelings, actions, or perceptions. Worrying about someone else's decisions or feelings will not change the outcome of the situation. Therefore this type of worrying is entirely unproductive. It only increases your stress and tension.

Learn to recognise when you're worrying about other people and let yourself let go.

"Worrying about other peoples actions gives you less time to focus on making yourself happy"
Unknown

2.) When you are overcome with feelings.

Often times, worry acts like a mask covering other feelings such as sadness and disappointment. This type of worry is especially prominent following a negative experience with others. For example, if you have recently gone through a break up, you might find yourself in a constant state of "worry" about what your ex-partner is doing, who they are seeing, what they are thinking or saying. In a case like this, worry is really just masking more difficult emotions. In the short term, this type of worry is covering up feelings of sorrow or grief but in the long term it may be
aggravating them leading you to longer lasting grief.

The only way to let go of worry such as this is by allowing yourself to feel your feelings. When a feeling of hurt or sadness rises up inside you, try not to wipe it away with worry or anxiety. Allow yourself to feel it. Know that it will not last forever. Recognise your feelings. Let them wash over you. Feel them and let them go.

Feelings are a part of life. No matter who you are, you will have them. Try picturing your feelings in the palm of your hand. Worrying acts like a closed fist. It keeps your difficult emotions trapped. Imagine walking through life with an open hand. Feelings will come to you, they will rest in the palm of your hand. But eventually they will leave you and with an open hand, they will do so without a struggle.

"He was swimming in a sea of other people's expectations and his own worries. Men had drowned in seas like that."
Robert Jordan

3.) When you've done all you can do.

Sometimes even after you've done everything can possibly do to shape the outcome of a situation, you still allow worry to ruminate inside you and disturb your peace. Remember, you cannot control the future, but you can control your worry. It is important to recognise when your worrying is getting the better of you. If you find that you are worrying about something for a prolonged period of time ask yourself "Have I done all I can do?". If the answer is yes, you need to say NO to your worry.

Tell yourself you have done all you can do, allow yourself to let go, and move on. You may need to tell yourself over and over but this will get easier with practice so don't give up and let your worry back in. Get in control and let go.

"Thinking will not overcome fear but action will."
W. Clement Stone

4.) When you are concerned about illness or death.

Worrying about falling ill or dying is extremely common. It is hard to ignore your mortality and the possibility that you may become ill at some point in your life. However, becoming overly anxious about it will not prevent it from happening. It is therefore, not worth zapping your energy or giving up your happiness for it. Worrying about dying might only prevent you from living.

In your life, you can't keep yourself from dying, but you can do things to keep fit. Eat healthy, get plenty of exercise, fresh air, and relaxation. Worrying won't do anything for you in this instance. It will only take from you. If do you fall ill, focus on what you can control rather than worrying about possible outcomes. The only thing you can control is your attitude. You can deal with illness by tackling it with determination or lying down in defeat. But no matter what decision you make, or what attitude you take, worrying will not change the outcome.

"Let us be of good cheer, remembering that the misfortunes hardest to bear are those that never happen."

James Russel Lowell

Step Three: Treat Your Worry Like A "To Do List"

When you are worrying, you are obsessing over possible future outcomes. The more time you spend thinking, the less you are actually doing. Turning your worry into something proactive will help you grasp the reality of your worries and help you gain control over them.

"Every day brings a choice: to practice stress or to practice peace"
Joan Borysenko

Generally speaking, people get a lot out of "to do lists", they can be highly effective. You write a list of things you need at the shops or things you must accomplish by the end of the day and each time you strike something off the list you naturally feel lighter and more positive.

Worry and anxiety can be abstract by nature. They don't necessarily have a shape or size and for this reason they may seem bigger than you from time to time. Moreover as you know, worrying can seem never ending. This is why treating your worry like a to do list works so well. It's not exactly easy to "switch off" excessive worrying so sometimes it's better to actually allow yourself to worry (in a controlled fashion!). The following exercise encourages you to visualize your problems, prioritize them, and develop a positive outcome from them.

Your Worry To Do List: Taking Action Today!

1.) Write down everything you are worried about. No matter how big or how small, even if it seems quite insignificant and silly.

2.) Prioritize your list. Ask yourself how serious each item on your list is. Put the most important things at the top of the list and follow those with less important concerns.

3.) DO what you can and do it TODAY.
Look over your list of worries and see if there are any ways you can ACT on them. For instance, are you worried about a faulty appliance in your kitchen potentially causing a fire? If so, call an electrician and STRIKE IT OFF YOUR LIST OF WORRIES. Once you have acted on something and crossed off your list, do not allow yourself to worry about it any longer as it has been taken care of. Done! Move on!

4.) Be productive with your worry. If there are things on your list that cannot be dealt with immediately via action, set a timer allow yourself to think about each problem for one to three minutes only. During that time, write down any actions you could take to ease your worry. If you can't think of any action or your time runs out, STRIKE IT OFF YOUR LIST.

5.) Be persistent. If you find that worries you have already crossed off your list are rising up in you again, refer back to your list, see that it is crossed off, and let go of it again. Silencing worried minds takes practice. Having a visual aid to remind you that you've done all you can do will help you let go of your worry and get on with your life.

"Do you remember the things you were worrying about a year ago? How did they work out? Didn't you waste a lot of fruitless energy on account of most of them? Didn't most of them turn out all right after all?"
Dale Carnegie

Step Four: Stop Worry In Its Tracks

By the time you reach this step in letting go of worry, you should feel a little more confident about gaining control about your thoughts. These things do take practice but, like any new skill, the more you put into it, the more you'll get out of it. Be sure to go over these exercises on a regular basis. Believe me, they work! This final step is one you can use whenever you feel worry creeping back into your life. The focus here is on positive perspective.

5 Steps To Freeing Yourself From Worry Immediately

1.) Recognise when you are worrying. You know that feeling when you know worry is creeping up? Recognise it!

2.) Quickly tell yourself to STOP. Grab the reins and steady your thoughts. Remember that your worries do not control you, you control them. You can take the control back!

3.) Get out of your head and into your body. Physical activity is a fantastic tool for getting the mind out of damaging thought cycles and refocused on life. Clean your house, go for a walk, go to the gym, play with your children, tidy your cupboards or your desk. Engage in any activity other than worrying.

4.) Get out. Do not underestimate the power of a change of scenery. Getting out in the sun, taking a walk in a new or interesting place, getting fresh air and exercise are an integral part of gaining perspective and resting your mind.

5.) Breathe. While you are out, stand still or sit down from time to time and let yourself breathe. Listen to the sounds around you. Feel the open air. Picture how far the world expands outside of you. Feel the breeze on your skin and focus on its sensation. Think of the other lifeforms living around you. Picture your worry in the expanse of this wide open space. Imagine how small it is here, how insignificant. Think of it as small and light as a leaf barely clinging to a winter tree. A leaf is not strong enough to shake the tree it clings to. Eventually it will fall and fly away. Imagine your worry falling away from you. Hold on to this perspective as you walk through life.

"Worry pretends to be necessary but serves no useful purpose"
Eckhart Tolle

The 5 Step Model To Letting Go Of Worry & Anxiety

Let's now look at another methodology for letting go of worry and anxiety, one which I have been using with my clients for the past decade with huge success.

Step One: Put a label on worrying thoughts
The first step is to identify when the phenomenon of worry is happening. Most worriers have worries around several similar themes, such as health, their job, relationships and finances. Because people see their worries as facts, it can be hard to distinguish a normal thought from a worry thought.

Worry thoughts typically follow patterns such as "what if" thoughts (e.g., "What if I'm terminally sick?" "What if I faint?") and ruminations. When people ruminate, they typically think and worry about the past, sometimes strongly wishing that they could go back in time and make a different decision. People also can ruminate around the word "Why." For instance, you might ask yourself "Why is that today there's a torrent of traffic?" or "Why does this have to happen to me of all people?"
Labeling your worry thoughts lets you know when to apply the model, and helps you start separating yourself from these thoughts.

Step Two: Let go of the reigns!
Step two encourages worriers to slow down the fight-or-flight response and relax the body by using stress management techniques such as breathing deeply and relaxing your hands and all your muscles, one at a time.
This is not so that you gain control over your anxiety as often attempting to overpower worry only extends anxiety and worry thoughts. The aim is to allow acceptance and mindfulness to enter, to recognize how you are feeling.

Step Three: Discover how you are feeling

The goal is to look at your worry thought instead of looking through it. That is, you begin viewing these thoughts as separate from yourself, a different entity. You remind yourself that your thoughts are not reality. They're not actual events. They are not real. They do not actually exist.
The aim is not to try to rid yourself of these thoughts but you're trying to distance yourself from them.

Step Four: The present moment
Practice mindfulness. At it's most basic, mindfulness means getting out of your head and being aware of your immediate surroundings, using all your senses. You do this in a nonjudgmental and compassionate away. You are not trying to deal with your thoughts, you are simply trying to fully recognize and accept them.

Step Five: Moving in the right direction
Worry takes us out of the moment and away from connecting with the way we want to move forward. We become focused on what could happen, often distorting reality. Oftentimes, we find ourselves placating our anxiety. Our anxiety might drive many of our choices. In fact, our anxiety might drive our lives.
Instead, the key is to make conscious choices based on your values. Values propel people forward, and give us a rationale or purpose for proceeding, even while anxiety is present.

Let's use the example of sailing a boat. Consider that the journey in the boat is your life, and you've got two instruments: a compass and a barometer. When you focus on anxiety, it's like you're steering the boat with a barometer, which provides you with the weather, not the direction. Using a barometer means you avoid any potential bad weather and you sail where the waters are calm. But using it to steer the ship also gives you no sense of direction. The compass, however, represents your values. When you use the compass, you know where you're going, even if the water is rough or the weather is dicey - or you're experiencing anxiety or difficult emotions.

In this section, you have learned how to identify the underlying thoughts to your worry. You have learned how to recognise when things are out of your control and let go of them. You have been encouraged to tackle your worries like a to do list. You've learned how to prioritize your worries and how act on them rather than letting them old you down. Finally, this section has given you the skills you need to keep your worry in perspective and let go of it for good!

Excessive worrying is thinking rooted in a future you cannot control. It is unhelpful and is holding you back from living the life you have in the here and now. It may take some practice, but soon you and your life will be free of the stifling grips of worry!

Part Two: Embarrassment & Shame. The Hidden Curses.

"Remembering that I'll be dead soon is the most important tool I've ever encountered to help me make the big choices in life. Because almost everything – all external expectations, all pride, all fear of embarrassment or failure – these things just fall away in the face of death, leaving only what is truly important"
Steve Jobs

Embarrassment is a self-conscious emotion similar to - and often intertwined with - guilt, shame, and pride. Embarrassment is a feeling that generally only occurs in relation to other people. For instance, if you are giving a speech at a wedding and you lose your train of thought or accidentally spill your drink over yourself, you will probably feel embarrassed, whereas if you were on your own and the same thing occurred you would be highly unlikely to feel the same way; as such, you can see that embarrassment loves an audience.

The individual nature of self-conscious emotions can make them difficult to fully categorize and interpret. Unlike your eye color or height which are determined by genetics and are relatively easy to explain, how a person experiences self-conscious emotions is based entirely on their individual lives and the experiences they have had. In order to feel these emotions a person must have standards for oneself, some ideas of what constitutes as failure, and the capacity to understand one's own behaviour and their effect on the world around them. But as you can imagine, these things will vary from person to person.

Each of us has beliefs about how we should behave in certain social situations. When you experience embarrassment you are viewing yourself within a public forum and through the eyes of other people. You see how you fit or don't fit into the world around you. You become aware of your separateness. You may feel exposed or awkward. You evaluate yourself through the eyes of others based on your understanding of social standards. Following an embarrassing moment, your mind can spiral into unhelpful thoughts or negative feelings about yourself that can be hard to let go of. This can then lead to worry, as dealt with in the first part of this book.

"The embarrassment of a situation can, once you are over it, be the funniest time in your life."
Miranda Hart

Though embarrassment is a natural human emotion, it can be emotionally dangerous and may hold you back in life. You might find that you can't stop thinking about an embarrassing moment, rerunning it in your head, or imagining how you could've done better. It can be a vicious circle, one that sometimes appears impossible to escape from. You may end up beating yourself up for something you said or did rather than just accepting it as an experience and moving on with life. You may find that memories of embarrassing moments rise up inside you when you are in social situations and make you feel anxious or uncomfortable. You may develop a fear of embarrassment that becomes a limiting force in your life. If you can't let go of embarrassment, you may end up with lowered self esteem, feelings of low self worth, social anxiety, depression, or countless other things that could hold you back from truly enjoying your life to its fullest.

"Courage starts with showing up and letting ourselves be seen."
Brene Brown

The next section is going to uncover what embarrassment is, where it comes from, and how it often works in tandem with guilt, shame, and pride. It will then equip you with the skills to let go of it for good!

Dealing With The Embarrassment People Feel

All individuals act differently in situations and react differently to stimuli. How they view themselves in situations informs whether they feel guilt, shame, embarrassment or none of the above. Early experiences very much shape how one evaluates their own behaviour in terms of success and failure. Failures in early life could lead to narcissistic disorders. So too, our early experiences of punishment and reward inform how we judge our achievements and our losses in later life.

Embarrassing moments occur when some aspect of yourself is revealed or threatens to be revealed in a forum where you would rather it didn't. These experiences are almost always accidental and they occur when you have no intention of drawing attention to yourself or of violating a social standard. Embarrassing experiences may be trips and falls, spilling drinks, unwelcome bodily functions, having your private thoughts or feelings exposed, and countless other accidents or occurrences that draw unwanted attention to yourself. Each of these events will produce a different level of embarrassment in each person. The reason one tends to feel embarrassed by occurrences such as these very common ones, is that they feel that the accident or exposure undermines the image of the self they seek to project. Meaning, if you seek to appear poised and professional when speaking in public and later find out that you had lipstick on your teeth or a bit of toilet paper attached to your shoe, you will feel that that accident undermines the image you had intended to put forth. You may then feel embarrassment and shame which could lead you to avoid a similar situation in the future. This is not a healthy way to live!

"You'll always miss 100% of the shots you don't take."
Wayne Gretzky

An interesting thing to note is that an incident or behaviour you find embarrassing in one context or in front of certain people, will not necessarily be embarrassing in a different context (such as when you are at home or in the company of a sibling, partner, or close friend). Picture yourself in the company of a boss or professor acting as you would with your brother and you can see that social context plays a big role in embarrassment.

Another interesting thing to note is that one person can be embarrassed on behalf of another. This is loosely called "second hand embarrassment". If you are in the company of someone who experiences a moment of embarrassment, you may feel equally embarrassed, awkward, or uncomfortable. This feeling may increase when you are in the company of someone superior like a boss or professor. Imagine having a meeting with your boss and noticing that their zip is down. You might feel a surge of embarrassment on their behalf. You may feel uncomfortable because you aren't sure if you should mention it or not and you may become flushed and distracted. The same goes for feeling embarrassed by the company you're in. Whether it's a loudmouthed mother-in-law, a tactless friend, or your tantruming niece, you may be the one experiencing the embarrassment from their behaviour. Thus, even if you hold no personal blame, you may still feel someone else's embarrassment or shame vicariously or due to your association with them.

Embarrassment And Guilt

Feelings of guilt often present in tandem with feelings of embarrassment. Unlike shame which focuses very much on societal moral standards (I will discuss shame in detail in the next section), guilt occurs when one feels as if they've fallen short of their own moral standards. Thus, guilt is very much focused on the self rather than how others view us. For instance, you may feel guilty about doing something nice for yourself such as buying yourself a nice bottle of perfume or eating a whole box of chocolates whereas these things might be perfectly acceptable in the eyes of another.

Most feelings of guilt are tied directly to a feeling of responsibility for someone else's pain, sickness, or misfortune; however, these feelings can be present even when you are not to blame. People who experience persistent feelings of guilt become convinced that they are to blame for other people's negative experience because they chronically mistaken themselves as being a cause of harm to others.

Feelings such as these can be extremely difficult to live with as it may be difficult or impossible for the person to understand or accept that they are not to blame.

"Guilt is cancer. Guilt will confine you, torture you, destroy you as an artist. It's a black wall. It's a thief."
Dave Grohl

Guilt is tied very closely to feelings of embarrassment in that it is both similar in nature and may also be more harmful than helpful. Guilt can also be, in itself, a cause of embarrassment. Therefore, if you want to be able to let go of embarrassment for good, you will also need to address your relationship with guilt. The following list should help you identify some ways you may experience guilt and help you address feelings of that are causing you more harm than good.

Addressing Guilty Feelings

1. True Guilt
True guilt is guilt you feel for something you actually did wrong which you would never want to do again. This might be the result of causing harm to someone else (physically or emotionally) or because you have violated your own moral or social standards (such as drinking too much or being aggressive). Feeling guilt over an action that is deserving of remorse is normal; however, if you are prone to rumination, your guilt may become bigger than you. You may become too focused on it and it may end up causing you more grief than is good for you. People often place too much importance on their own thoughts and actions which means after the incident, you may be the only one still thinking about it. It is important to remember that no matter what the circumstance, it is almost always not as bad as it seems to you.

2. Fantasy Guilt
Fantasy guilt is about actions you haven't actually carried out but

which you are thinking about committing. These may be thing that are illegal, dishonest, or unfaithful. This type of guilt can be very difficult to cope with. Even if you haven't committed an act, you are still contemplating something that goes against your own moral code. Tackling these types of thoughts can be tricky but the best way to cope with this type of guilt is by recognising your taboo thoughts, doing your best not to act on them, and attempting to control your thoughts and desires as best as you can. Try to give yourself some slack and remember that thoughts are different from actions. You may not be able to control your thoughts but you can control whether or not you act upon them or not.

3. False Guilt
False guilt is when you believe you've done something wrong when in actuality, you haven't. This is often due to a belief that you have the power to "jinx" people or affect them negatively by thinking of them in a negative light (such as wishing harm on an ex-lover). Even if you know on some level that these beliefs are illogical, it can be hard to shift this type of guilt. Try to listen to your logical thoughts and challenge your guilt by asking yourself "how". I.e. "How is this my fault?" or "How have I caused this?".

4. "Never enough" Guilt
This is the type of guilt one experiences when they feel as if they haven't done enough to help someone in need. Ironically, this feeling is often experienced by people who are doing everything they possibly can to help other people. These people will feel like even if they've given up every available moment for years, they still should've offered more. This is a distortion of reality sometimes known as "compassion fatigue". If you are the type of person who offers endless support to others, it is important to prioritize yourself and your life. Try to separate your desire to help from your feelings of guilt or obligation and give yourself a break. Acting out of guilt will leave you drained, exhausted, and unhappy.

5. Survivor Guilt
Survivor guilt was originally classed as guilt felt by soldiers who outlived their fellow officers in times of war; however, that classification is by no means comprehensive. Survivor guilt also

characterizes guilt felt by those who have achieved more than their friends or family. This could be tied to a variety of situations such as getting into a better school than your classmates, landing a better job than your peers, or achieving any higher level of "success" than others. This type of guilt can make you want to hide your successes from others or may even lead you to self-sabotage. If you regularly experience survivor guilt, it is necessary to recognise that your achievements are yours. They are not a comment on others. You did not reach the level of success you hold because you wanted to make others feel badly. Whatever you own, you earned it and you deserve it. Most importantly, remind yourself regularly that your loved ones want you be happy and secure. They would not be happier if you were less successful.

"No work or love will flourish out of guilt, fear, or hollowness of heart, just as no valid plans for the future can be made by those who have no capacity for living now"
Alan Watts

Hopefully you can see how your feelings of guilt may be causing your feelings of embarrassment. Do you feel embarrassed when someone points out how well you're doing? Do you feel embarrassed if you feel you think you haven't put enough time or energy toward someone else's struggles even though you've given as much as you could? Do you feel embarrassed about something you have done that you wish you didn't? All of these, are examples of how guilt could be the underlying cause of your negative experience of embarrassment. You should be able to see how these feelings could contribute negatively to your feelings about yourself and your life.

Eradicate The Guilt!

Look over the 5 types of guilt above and write down a few that hit home with you. Which parts could you relate to, even if only slightly? Ask yourself if you are holding yourself back because of feelings of guilt? Is there something you did in your past that you haven't forgive yourself for or properly accepted? Are you the type of person that cares so much for others that you end up starving yourself of the same care?

Are you the type of person that feels like everything is your fault most of the time? Do you regularly disallow yourself to experience happiness, love, or affection because of deep rooted feelings of guilt about something in your past, even if that something was out of your control?

Do not rush this. Take some time to reflect on your feelings of guilt and embarrassment. Really allow yourself to feel it. Think about ways these feelings are holding you back in life. Think of actual real life examples. Think about how these feelings make you feel about yourself. Think about how these feelings shape your relationships with others in the past or people in your life now.

Once you have done this, ask yourself if there are any positive effects of your guilt. Then ask yourself if there are any negative effects of it. Write down your answers in as much detail as you can. This can take time but it is VITAL in order to recognize your feelings and move on.

"There's no regret. You can't regret. I mean, I've felt regret but I've also refused to allow regret to sow a seed and live in me because I don't believe it. You feel it, it's like guilt, it's like jealousy, it's like all those horrible thoughts. You've just got to snip them and get them out, because they're no good."
Jude Law

Embarrassment And Shame: Overcome and Progress

Embarrassment and shame are so closely related they are often mistaken for one another but there are some subtle but important differences. Feelings of shame are related to negative evaluations of the self. Both embarrassment and shame have serious effects on human dignity and can thus have negative effects on your self esteem and your overall happiness in life.

Whereas guilt is usually centered on one's own beliefs of how they should behave, shame is linked more closely to one's moral character as viewed in a social context. Shame arises when one compares themselves to societal norms and feels that they have fallen short. These feelings are particularly prevalent in people with low self esteem and poor self image. People who judge themselves harshly often struggle with shame as they become focused on what they have not yet achieved or they believe their life should be better than it is. Those who have recently lost something such as money, a job, or a relationship are may be prone to heightened feelings of shame.

Feelings of shame are amongst the weightiest types of embarrassment. Though, in small doses, shame might lead you toward a more moral lifestyle, in large doses it can have horrible impacts on your life. Shame can become intertwined with feelings of self-blame and contempt and can lead to deeper shame and an even lower self esteem.

A person experiencing high amounts of shame might become isolated due to feelings of low self worth. They may steer away from close relationships and limit themselves in a multitude of ways. For instance, a person who experienced financial success and subsequently lost it, may end up becoming so focused on their downfall (and the shame that came attached to it) that they disallow any happiness to enter their life until they regain their previous financial position. One might place unnecessary limits on their lives and alienate oneself from others because deep down, they feel they don't deserve nice things, vacations, or the love and affection from others. This type of behaviour can lead to feelings of deep and long-lasting dissatisfaction, self-loathing, lowered self confidence, and loneliness. Feelings of shame - whether they are based on a financial collapse or a succession of bad relationships - may cause a person to go through multiple short term relationships due to a fear of others finding out who or what they "really are". They may end relationships abruptly, even when things are going well because they are afraid of failing again. They are trying to protect themselves.

"Fear: False Evidence Appearing Real."
Unknown

You can imagine how someone with deep rooted shame might keep others at arm's length and how that guarded behaviour might shape their present and future happiness. If these feelings aren't addressed, one might spend their entire life isolated from others. They might not be able to accept another person's love or admiration. They might habitually deflect compliments or respect from others. This type of under confident behaviour will likely repel potential friends or lovers and hence, rather than feeling protected from the judgment of others, the shame filled person will feel the effects of loss and self loathing again and again.

Realign Shameful Feelings

It is important to recognise feelings of shame that may be shaping your life in negative ways. If you regularly place limits on your life or your relationships with others you may be wasting your time on earth trying to become "better". Restrictions in your present may lead to depression, regret, lost opportunities, and deeper feelings of self-loathing in your future. Take some time to explore what negative feelings are shaping your life with the following exercise.

Write a list of limits you regularly place on yourself. Be honest when evaluating your life. Avoid making excuses or thinking about your reasons for doing so.

Look at your diet: Do you constantly place restrictions on what you eat or drink because of a lack of confidence or self worth?

Look at your belongings: Do you disallow yourself from purchasing nice things because you feel you don't deserve them?

Look at your schedule: Are you forcing yourself to work constantly because of a past failure you feel you can overcome by working harder?

Look at your social life: Do you regularly make excuses to not go out because you are ashamed or embarrassed of yourself or your life?

Look at your relationships: Do you back away from love or affection because you feel you don't deserve it? Do you place limitations on your relationships so you will not have to expose your true self to others? Do you go through a succession of short term relationships? Do you place rules and restrictions on your relationships? Do you regularly end relationships even then they are going well because you're afraid of how they might turn out in the end?

Look at your list of restrictions and ask yourself why. Remember, <u>you are doing this for you and your potential happiness</u> so there is no good in lying to yourself! Let go of your usual excuses and reasons and dig deeper. In order to free yourself from the restraints of embarrassment and ensure happiness and contentment in your life, you must be willing to stand up to your most honest self.

Write your answers down and reflect on them over the coming days and weeks. Keep your list close by so you can look over it regularly. Look over it after you spend time with others and try to recognise patterns of being guarded or deflecting respect or affection. Look over it when you are stressed out by work and ask yourself if you are pushing too hard.

It is important to be an active participant in your life. Remember that feelings of shame and embarrassment are a negative force in your life. They are feelings that are holding you back and keeping you down. Figuring out why is the first step in ridding yourself of it.

"You gain strength, courage and confidence by every experience in which you really stop to look fear in the face. You must do the thing which you think you cannot do."
Eleanor Roosevelt

Embarrassment And Pride

The final type of embarrassment I am going to discuss is the type you feel when you are actually proud of yourself or your accomplishments. This might seem a bit far fetched, but most people have experienced this type of embarrassment at some point in their lives, even if they did not fully realize it at the time.

Unlike the type of embarrassment that occurs when something dreadful happens to you in public, pride-based embarrassment occurs when something good happens to you. Imagine winning a raffle draw and having to go up and collect your prize in front of a crowd. You may feel your cheeks flush and you might want to claim your prize and run! Imagine you achieve a high success in work or at school and your superior praises you in front of your co-workers or classmates. You may feel embarrassed even though you are being praised for something you worked very hard to achieve. A similar embarrassment might be felt when someone simply tells you that you look good on a day you've spent extra time doing your hair or choosing your outfit. You might immediately negate the compliment, hide your face, or tug at your clothes because you feel embarrassed by the attention despite the positive nature of it.

This type of embarrassment is paradoxical because it is almost always felt in regards to something you intentionally worked hard for; however, receiving recognition for it makes you feel exposed, self conscious, or uncomfortable.

Another form of pride-based embarrassment is that which is felt when you have achieved more highly than a friend someone in your family such as a sibling or a parent. You may feel inclined to hide your achievements or lie about things such as your annual income or your recent promotion to a sibling who hasn't experienced the same level of success as you. If your parent was less educated or financially stable than you are, you may feel embarrassed when the topic arises with them, especially when in the company of others.

Though this type of embarrassment seems the most obscure, it is actually very common, and for that reason it's a great example of how embarrassment can hold you back in life and cause negative feelings about yourself. If you are unable to recognise your own achievements, your own hard work, and your own praiseworthy attributes, you may be robbing yourself of respect (from both yourself and others), preventing your own future success, and disallowing yourself to feel any sense of self-satisfaction or self-love.

The next part of this book will show you some ways you can attack your embarrassment and free yourself from it for good. But before moving on here's a short recap of what you have learned about embarrassment so far.

1.) Embarrassment in a natural self conscious emotion that varies from person to person. It is most often felt in the presence of others as a result of some comparison of yourself to them.

2.) Embarrassment is a negative evaluation of the self. It is rooted in guilt, shame, or pride which may lead to low self esteem and harmful self-beliefs.

3.) Embarrassment may lead to unhelpful ruminating thoughts such as rerunning an unpleasant moment over and over again in your head. Such indulgences are counteractive in life. They can be harmful to your mood and may cause excessive fear and worry that may hold you back in the future.

4.) Embarrassment has such negative effects on your self beliefs that it has the power to hold you back from positive experiences in your career, your relationships, your overall outlook on life, your self esteem, and your true potential.

"Never be afraid to try something new. Remember amateurs built the ark, professionals built the Titanic."
Unknown

Letting Go Of Embarrassment: Live a Happy Life!

You are now well aware of the damaging effects of embarrassment. You know that it is holding you back. You know embarrassment is causing you unnecessary social anxiety and that it's easily turned into a weapon of self destruction. Now it's time to focus on letting go of embarrassment for good. This section will walk you through 3 steps to freeing yourself from the grips of embarrassment.

Step One: The Underlying Belief

Embarrassment highlights negative beliefs about yourself. These may be things about you that were exaggerated in a single moment or they may be deep rooted feelings of shame or guilt still lingering from somewhere in your past. You might experience obsessive rumination that focuses on negative feelings about yourself. You may replay an embarrassing moment over and over in your head, like a film reel on an endless loop.

Interestingly, these types of thoughts tend to strike most when you are already in a period of low mood. For instance, if you are feeling embarrassed about something you did in front of another person five minutes ago, you may start to relive another time in your life when something similar happened. Your mind sometimes creates a link – often an unrealistic and unhelpful link. Another example of this is if you told a friend that you are in love with someone and that person later rejects you, you might feel embarrassed and ashamed that you were so open about your feelings. You may feel foolish. In that moment, you may relive past experiences of rejection and shame. Rather than seeing this experience as a single isolated incident, you believe it to be something much larger. You feel a lifetime of rejection and shame. This "snowball effect" of embarrassment and shame provide you with further reason to loath and limit yourself.

"Fear is only as deep as the mind allows."
Japanese Proverb

In this way you can see how a moment of embarrassment can trigger memories past experiences of embarrassment and exaggerate your feelings in the here and now. In order to cope better with embarrassment in your present, you must identify the underlying self beliefs still lingering from your past. The following list illustrates some harmful underlying self beliefs that could be exaggerating your embarrassment.

4 Common Experiences That Exaggerate Embarrassment

1.) Grief

Experiences of grief and loss can be very hard to shift. Many people think that grief is only something experienced following the death of a loved one, however that is not the case at all. People experience grief for a variety of reasons such as the loss of a friendship, the end of a relationship, the loss of a job or social standing, and many other things. If you feel responsible for the ending of something, your grief could be exaggerating your feelings of embarrassment. Grief that goes unrecognized or unaddressed could antagonize you. For instance, if you once lost a job that you continue to grieve and dwell on, you may become painful embarrassed or ashamed if something goes wrong in your current job, even if only a small and quite insignificant thing.

Ask yourself if grief from your past is exaggerating your feelings of embarrassment or shame in your present. Address those moments in your past. Let yourself think about them and feel the loss. Then encourage yourself to leave that experience in the past. You will remember it from time to time but try to remind yourself that each new experience in life is new, not an extension of the experiences in your past. Accept and move on.

"I am not afraid of tomorrow, for I have seen yesterday and I love today!"
William Allen White

2.) Guilt

As I discussed above, guilt can be tightly woven into your experiences of embarrassment. If you believe everything is your fault you are acting as your worst enemy. In order to let go of guilt you must address why you feel so guilty. Did you do something that you wish you hadn't? Do you place too much attention on others and not enough on yourself? Do you believe you deserve less than other people? Do you constantly believe that you are at fault? Do you feel bad about being more successful than a parent, sibling, or close friend?

Take some time to identify any feelings of guilt that might be exaggerating your embarrassment. Encourage yourself to let go of guilt that is holding you back. The key to letting go of guilt is forgiving and accepting yourself. Everyone makes mistakes in life. EVERYONE! Recognise when it's time to forgive yourself and let go of guilt for good. Treat yourself like you would treat a friend. Tell yourself that you deserve happiness and good things in life. Remember that these things won't disappear overnight but regular self-talk will ultimately lead you to being free of guilt. It is important to practice these principles everyday until they become second nature.

"I must not fear.
Fear is the mind-killer.
Fear is the little-death that brings total obliteration.
I will face my fear.
I will permit it to pass over me and through me.
And when it has gone past I will turn the inner eye to see its path.
Where the fear has gone there will be nothing.
Only I will remain.
Secure.

Safe.
Happy."
Frank Herbert

3.) Under-achievements

If you have a tendency to focus more on your under-achievements and losses in life, each time you experience a downfall your embarrassment about it will be heightened. You may have unhelpful thoughts like, "I've messed up again.", "I always lose" or "I'll never get anything right". Focusing on under-achievements such as unhealthy relationships in your past, financial losses, mistakes in your education or career, or constant feelings of achieving "less" than others is not only damaging to your self esteem, it will also cause you to view any further mistakes in an overblown way.
The more attached you are to your past under-achievements, the more embarrassed you will be the next time something goes wrong. Leave you under-achievements in the past! Forgive yourself, accept the loss, and move on. Now is now. Leave the past behind!

"You make a decision that you are going to move on. It won't happen automatically. You will have to rise up and say, "I don't care how hard this is, I don't care how disappointed I am, I'm not going to let this get the best of me. I'm moving on with my life."
Joel Osteen
<u>Your Best Life Now: 7 Steps To Living At Your Full Potential</u>

4.) Success

The idea of success is different to everyone. Whether it's money or happiness, relationships or travels, if you focus too much on the idea of success, you may be putting yourself in direct competition with other people (or yourself). This might mean never allowing yourself to feel good about your accomplishments, or being too hard on yourself when you haven't reached a certain goal. In addition, if you have once had "success" in your life and subsequently lost it, you may put too much pressure on yourself to reach that level of success again. This could mean feeling overly embarrassed or ashamed at every pitfall along the way.

Overall, goal setting in life is good. However, do your best to accept that every journey will have good points and bad. Resist the urge to judge yourself based on the successes of your peers. Let go of any negative feelings you may have from a past success. Give yourself credit every time you overcome or achieve something rather than beating yourself up every time things go wrong.

"You will find that it is necessary to let things go; simply for the reason that they are heavy. So let them go, let go of them. I tie no weights to my ankles"
C. JoyBell C.

Step Two: Be Graceful About It And Keep It In Perspective

A large part of coping with feelings of embarrassment is how you manage them "in the moment". If you are prone to replaying embarrassing moments over and over in your head, knowing you handled an embarrassing moment gracefully will help keep you from obsessing over it. So too, you must keep your embarrassing moments in perspective. When embarrassing experiences are allowed to take over your thoughts they can have detrimental effects on your self beliefs and your behaviour.

"No one saves us but ourselves. No one can say and no one may. We ourselves walk the path."
Buddha

In order to keep your embarrassment from taking over, refer to the following list on a regular basis. Many people find it useful to read this every morning for the first few weeks of this new journey.

5 Fundamental Truths About Embarrassment

1.) You are not alone.

Take comfort in the fact that everyone gets embarrassed! Many of your earliest memories will be rooted in embarrassments that happened in school or at the playground and the same goes for most people. Embarrassment is a normal human experience and though it may feel horrible at the time, it is ultimately insignificant. You have to let it go.

2.) Your embarrassment doesn't define you.

No matter what has happened, you must remind yourself that you are not defined by your embarrassments. Whether you have said something stupid or made a mistake in your career, you are more than these things. To help keep your embarrassment in perspective, think of how a person close to you might describe you to other people. Would you best friend tell describe you by telling someone that you once had toilet paper on your shoe or would they say you are kind, funny, and generous? Would your friends describe you by saying you're always messing up or would they say you've had some hard times but you always rise to a challenge?

Remember: No matter what embarrassment has been to you, it has not been your defining feature.

3.) No one else remembers your embarrassment.

No matter what caused your embarrassment, it is highly likely that no one else remembers it happening. And if they do, they don't care about it. REALLY! You can rest assured knowing that you're thinking about your embarrassment more than anyone else is, because everyone else is remembering their own embarrassment. Studies have shown that after a night out, people rarely remember much outside of their own experience. They remember how they were feeling, what they said, what they wore, how they looked in the mirror in the restroom, and how they believe they were perceived.

Therefore, the only person affected by your embarrassment is you. You can either let it go or use it to torture yourself with. (I recommend letting go of it…)

4.) There is no place for ego where embarrassment is concerned.

One of the best things you can do to protect yourself from the harmful effects of embarrassment is to let go of your ego. Try not to engage with high levels of competition with others and you may prevent yourself from feeling unnecessarily high levels of social discomfort. In other words, when something embarrassing happens, be graceful about it. Acknowledge it, smile, and laugh about it. Everyone has been embarrassed so even if your friends poke and prod you about it, they know how you're feeling. Being graceful will not only help you feel better about it, but other people will respect you and ultimately like you more. A problem shared is a problem halved. With embarrassment, there is safety in numbers!

5.) No one has ever died of embarrassment!

Keep it in perspective! If you are replaying an embarrassing moment over and over in your head, ask yourself what purpose it's serving. Resist the urge to hurt yourself by reminding yourself of an embarrassing moment. Don't let a moment in your past anchor you and harm your self beliefs. Lighten up and let go of it. Your embarrassment happened in the past. It does not define your present or your future. No embarrassment is worth holding on to. It serves no purpose.

Step Three: Turn It Into Something Positive, Fast!

Sometimes it's hard to let go of embarrassment no matter how much positive "self talk" you practice, that's why this step can be so effective. You know the negative effects of embarrassment but you might feel like it's not enough just knowing that it serves no purpose. You might still feel plagued or weighed down by it. If you feel like knowledge isn't enough to battle your embarrassment, give it a purpose. Use the following tips to turn your embarrassment into something positive.

3 Ways To Make Your Embarrassment Positive

1.) Make it useful.

Give your embarrassment a purpose by letting it help you learn and grow. Instead of beating yourself about embarrassing mistakes, think about some ways you can prevent them from happening again in the future. If you are embarrassed or ashamed of a loss, use that experience to help you make better decisions next time. Rather than letting your embarrassments hold you back, let them propel you forward. Don't let embarrassments force you to avoid life, make them push you to tackle life head on. Avoidance solves nothing and holds you back.

If you had bad relationships in the past, don't avoid them in your future, just learn from them and do better next time. You deserve love and affection.

If you made mistakes in your career life, don't bury your head in the sand and stop trying. Learn from your mistakes, make a plan, and go for it. You deserve to feel fulfilled by your career.

If you let people down in the past, don't use that as an excuse to push people away. Trust that you have grown from your experience and start letting people in again. You deserve companionship and fun.

"A pessimist sees the difficult in every opportunity; an optimist sees the opportunity in every difficulty."
Winston Churchill

2.) Practice decreasing shame.

Shame can have a vice like grip on you. That's why getting rid of it takes time and practice. A lot of times, you may be acting as your own worst enemy so when it comes to decreasing your feelings of shame, it can be beneficial to talk to yourself like you would talk to a friend. When your thoughts spiral into unhelpful memories or beliefs, be a friend to yourself. Would you tell a friend they should feel ashamed? Or would you tell them to let go of their shame and move on? If a friend was holding back from trying new things because of shame would you tell them to keep living in the past or would you encourage them to make some steps toward a happy, vibrant and productive future? If your friend was constantly punishing himself, would you join in? Or would you encourage him to forgive himself?

Practice decreasing shame by practicing positive and helpful "self talk" whenever you notice yourself being your own worst enemy. Allow yourself room for error. Be free to just be!

"The world is round and the place which may seem like the end may also be only the beginning."
Ivy Baker Priest

3.) Seek less competition.

If you are constantly comparing yourself to others (or to your past self) you will never be happy. It is important to stop judging yourself with unreasonably high standards. Set your own goals and judge yourself on your own criteria. Seek less competition and you will find yourself feeling more peaceful and positive.

"We can complain because rose bushes have thorns, or rejoice because thorn bushes have roses."
Abraham Lincoln

In this section you have learned about a variety of causes and effects of embarrassment. You have learned how to identify underlying thoughts that could be exaggerating your feelings of embarrassment and shame. You have learned how positive "self talk" is necessary to break free from the confines of embarrassment. You have learned how to gain and maintain perspective about embarrassment and how to turn your embarrassment into something positive.

Embarrassment is rooted in the past but if allowed to, it can stifle your experience in the present and the future. Embarrassment and shame can have detrimental effects to your self image and your sense of self worth. In order to keep your present and your future bright, leave all that has passed in the past, where it belongs.
Live in the now.
Life for the present.

Eight Proven Ways To Overcome Embarrassment

1. Keep the right tense.
All embarrassment takes place in the past. Theoretically, if you were able to stay in the moment perfectly, you wouldn't feel an ounce of embarrassment – because all those messages inside your brain belong to a different time and place. Now I realize being present to the moment is virtually impossible when you are experiencing that twisted knot inside your stomach that says things like, "You can't be trusted with anything, you idiot!" and are feeling the physiological symptoms of embarrassment (somewhat like the flu), but if you can remember for even a minute here or there to pull your attention to the present, you will be relieved of needless angst.

2. Stop apologizing.
This one is counter-intuitive for me. I honestly think that if I apologize I will return to feeling normal. Even if I have apologized like five minutes prior to that moment. I suppose I am an apology addict. "Just one more apology and I'll feel okay." No. You won't. In fact, you will feel worse. Because, again, your attention is on the past, not on the present, where you don't need to apologize for anything. So stop it already.

3. Be you. Neurotic you.
St. Francis de Sales had four words of advice for pursuing spiritual excellence: "Be you very well." That even goes for neurotics, like me, who wear their psychiatric charts on their sleeves, and are so transparent that every thought they have is registered like a bulletin on their faces. I supposed when you are made that way – or, rather, if you choose to live that way – you will experience far more embarrassment than, say, a person who tucks away her emotions for only safe people to see. But if Francis is right, that's the price I have to pay for being me.

4. Visit humiliations past.
This one will help you keep things in perspective. You know when you thought you really were going to die – or at least you wanted to? In hindsight, not a huge deal, right? As an exercise, you should list

your top five embarrassments.

5. Laugh about it.
This one is easy in hindsight. I mean, embarrassment stories make great cocktail-party material!
But when you're in "sensitivity land," laughing is a tad challenging, which is why you need a good friend to help you with it. A few days ago I pulled up to a gas tank near my kids' school and discovered I was on the island with a flat tire, which did not help rumors that I was a bad driver.
"Do you think I'm a bad driver?" I asked a friend in tears.
"Hell, yes!" she said. "You drive like a grandma. There's no way in hell I'd get into your passenger side – BUT you can drive my kids anywhere you like!"
We laughed and suddenly I wasn't so afflicted by my driving reputation.

6. Allow some tilting.
Embarrassment belongs to the disorder known as perfectionism. Think about it. You are embarrassed because you didn't live up to your standards. There is a small (or wide) gap between your expectations of yourself and your performance. You will have some bad days. Accept that. Nobody is perfect.

7. Learn how to be afraid.
Embarrassment is essentially fear – of being perceived in a way that is less, well, endearing than we'd like. So we if learn how to be afraid, we can handle the embarrassment in a way that is more psychologically and physiologically tolerable. Taylor Clark, author of the book *Nerve*, gave me some simple instructions on how to handle fear in a recent interview I did with him:

While we can't instantly stop ourselves from getting startled or from feeling fear in response to the things that scare us, we do have the power to change how we relate to these emotions, which is all that counts. The more we learn to welcome our fear and anxiety, work with them, and weave them into the lives we want to lead, the less beholden we are to the whims of the amygdala [the brain's fear control center]. And eventually, with enough effort and patience, the conscious mind gains the power to say, "Hey, amygdala, I have this one under control."

8. Step away from the looking glass.
I once heard this expression: "I'm not who I think I am. Nor am I who you think I am. But I am who I think you think I am." I had to repeat it like four times before I got the gist. Most of the time we base our identity on what we think other people think of us

Part Three: Regrets & How To Move On

"We all make mistakes, have struggles, and even regret things in our past. But you are not your mistakes, you are not your struggles, and you are here NOW with the power to shape your day and your future."
Steve Maraboli
<u>Unapologetically You: Reflections on Life and the Human Experience</u>

When you think of how regret functions in your life, you may think of times you wish things had gone better. You may be reminded of a myriad of negative experiences in your past such as unhealthy relationships, missed opportunities, financial or familial mistakes, and anything else you feel like you could've or should've done better. But regret isn't just about remembering bad outcomes, it's about remembering them in a context where you are at fault. This ultimately leads to unhelpful thinking and harmful evaluations of self.

When you experience feelings of regret you are actively engaging in an emotional state of self-blame. This is where the true nature of regret becomes apparent. You dwell on experiences where you believe you let yourself or someone else down. You allow your feelings of loss or grief to take on a new shape; one wherein you are solely to blame. For this reason, regret can easily be turned into a weapon against yourself and become a toxic force in your life. You can use it to beat yourself up about almost any negative experience.

Regret is a tendency to view yourself as the cause of any (or every) undesirable outcome in your life. When you are in a state of regret you are not simply feeling the painful emotions of sadness, loss, or despair, you are also focusing your negative emotions toward yourself because you believe you should have, or could have, done better. Your thoughts may cycle into fantasies of how things might've been if you'd handled a situation differently. You might believe that things would have turned out better if you'd acted differently and this might lead to feelings of disappointment in yourself and life in general.

Thus, your negative emotions may end up taking over your thoughts, challenging your self-beliefs, and leading you down a path of self-loathing and hopelessness. If you are experiencing regret about things you cannot change, you may get caught in a loop of rumination and chronic stress which can have a detrimental effect on your relationships, career, physical health, and overall potential for happiness and contentment in your life.

How The World Around Us Feeds Regret & How To Stop It!

In today's world, advertising campaigns surround us at all times. Nowadays it's not just TV commercials and billboards dictating trends. Thanks to our smart phones, tablets, and laptops, most people spend the majority of their time "online". This means being bombarded with advertisements at work, at home, in transit, in the waiting room at the doctor's office, and basically everywhere else you spend your waking hours.

The more you are faced with ads telling you how you should be living, the more you will inevitably come to view your life choices as shortcomings rather than valuing your decisions and lifestyle. If you had someone constantly in your ear telling you that you should've eaten a healthier breakfast, you should've worn more expensive shoes, or you should've been married with children by now, you will soon start to believe these things and view yourself in a negative light. That is exactly what is happening when you are surrounded with advertisements. You are being forced to evaluate yourself through the eyes of marketing agencies. And why would they do this? To guilt you in to buying their products.

The same can be said for judgmental friends and family members. Is your mother-in-law overly critical of how you feed your children? Is your brother always nagging you about your annual income? Is your sister regularly pointing out the things you don't have? Unfortunately, even when family members have your best interest at heart, their passing comments can lead to long periods of rumination and self-doubt. If your friends are always dressed better than you or constantly bragging about their life choices around you, you may feel as if you are less successful than them and you may grow to regret your life decisions as a result. If you are constantly being compared to others, or actively comparing yourself to others, you may never learn to value yourself and your life. This could lead to regrets about your path of education, your romantic choices, your career progression, your decision to have children or not…absolutely anything and everything! The would around you could be arming you with a lot of emotional weaponry you can use against yourself. This needs to be dealt with. This *can* be dealt with!

Romantic Regrets

Regret is felt by everyone at some time or another, but what is it people regret most? As you might imagine, this toxic rumination does vary greatly in its source and generally speaking, it can affect women and men for different reasons. However, studies show that regardless of gender, romantic regrets are at the top of the list.

Studies show that women put increased value on relationships whereas men tend to "replace" romantic partners more quickly and thus spend less time and energy on romantic regrets; however, this is not to suggest that women are plagued with regret about lost lovers and men feel nothing. On the contrary, romantic regrets are felt by all and are almost always felt by both parties following a break up, regardless of who ended the relationship.

Romantic regrets can be the hardest ones to shift as one may feel pressured to be in a healthy relationship by friends, family, and co-workers. This could mean that a break-up doesn't just mean losing a partner, it may also mean losing your self confidence, your self worth, your hopes for the future, your self image, and myriad other things that may lead to depression and social withdrawal.

Furthermore, in today's society the "dating game" can be fast, furious, and impersonal. Ads for dating websites and casual sex apps are everywhere. In today's world, less attention is paid to romance and deep interpersonal connections while more attention is paid to the bedroom and the belief that being "single" is the most tragic thing that can happen in adult life. These influences may be causing both women and men to feel more romantic regrets than they would've done a few decades back when courting was slower and casual sex was less common. After all, romantic regret is not just felt at the end of meaningful relationships, it is also very commonly experienced after spending the night with someone you didn't know or respect or wasting time chatting to someone online who didn't turn out to be what you expected.

Another reason romantic regrets are at the top of the list is because these regrets can spur on feelings of rejection and abandonment. Rejection is among the hardest human emotions to experience. It is natural to feel good about yourself when you are being loved, appreciated, cared for, and respected. This is one of the reasons people seek relationships with others in the first place. When you're in a relationship, you feel like someone understands and accepts you. This does wonders for your self esteem and general quality of life. However, you may get into the habit of relying on a romantic partner to determine your self worth. A dangerous trap. You may feel great when they are paying attention to you and then find your mood plummets when their attention is elsewhere. Therefore, when a relationship ends and/or someone rejects you, all of the positive feelings you had about yourself when they were being attentive and caring may come to a tragic end. You may feel automatically forced to reevaluate yourself and you may become entirely focused on your own short comings. This happens often. Rather than thinking about the other person's reasons and issues for ending a relationship, one may focus solely on what they did wrong, what they are lacking, and why they aren't good enough. This is when regret is at its most harmful. Being faced with the end of a relationship will inevitably cause feelings of loss and grief, but add to that feelings of self-loathing and hopelessness, and you've got yourself a deadly cocktail that has the power to destruct life as you know it.

"Falling in love, romance, matters of the hear – when you fall in love, on some biochemical level you know there is a chance it won't work out. It's ingrained in us that if you take such an enormous risk on someone with your heart that it might not pay off. I gamble all my chips and I might actually lose everything. But I must believe that I won't."
Rachael Taylor

However it is very important to say that this is not to say that one should avoid attachment relationships in order to keep themselves emotionally "safe". On the contrary, research on how regret functions over time shows that though, in the short term, regrets tend to be focused on mistakes and actions taken, in the long term, regrets tend to focus on actions not taken. Surveys have shown that the majority of older adults regret few actions taken but have much stronger feelings of regret about not taking enough risks in life. That is to say, over longer periods of time, adults are more likely to regret missed opportunities for love, "missing" one's life by working too hard, and missed opportunities to spend time with friends and family. This is an interesting crossover point of regret and worry.

If you spend your time worrying about the future and limiting the choices you make and the chances you take now, you may end up regretting your past when it comes time to reflect back. You can see how focusing too much on the future or the past might lead to dissatisfaction and uneasiness in the present.

The Most Important Top Ten List You Will Ever Read

Top 10 Deathbed Regrets as contributed by Shannon L. Alder, author and therapist who has 17 years experience working with hospice patients.

1. I wish I'd had the courage to live a life true to myself, not the life other people expected of me.

2. I wish I took time to be with my children more when they were growing up.

3. I wish I had the courage to express my feelings, without the fear of being rejected or unpopular.

4. I wish I would have stayed in touch with friends and family.

5. I wish I would have forgiven someone when I had the chance. I wish I would have forgiven myself.

6. I wish I would have told the people I loved the most how important they are to me.

7. I wish I would have had more confidence and tried more things, instead of being afraid of looking like a fool.

8. I wish I would have done more to make an impact in this world.

9. I wish I would have experienced more, instead of settling for a boring life filled with routine, mediocrity and apathy.

10. I wish I would have pursued my talents and gifts.

(contributed by Shannon L. Alder, author and therapist that has 17 years of experience working with hospice patients)"

The Negative Effects Of Regret & How To Stop Them

Though regret can sometimes have positive effects on your life such as helping you prevent future mistakes or negative behaviours, more often than not, the effects of regret are negative and damaging and should be stopped. Regret often causes endless rumination which leads to harmful conclusions and a pattern of self-focused, repetitive thinking. The conclusions most often drawn from these unhelpful thought cycles are rooted in self-blame, self-loathing, and shame.

You cannot change things that happened in the past no matter how much you wish you could. When all of your thoughts are centered around something that happened in the distant or recent past, you may find yourself detached from life in the present. You may become disengaged with work or relationships. You may become withdrawn socially. You may become hopeless, deeply unhappy, or depressed. You may experience chronic stress and become less capable of coping with day to day life. Furthermore, ruminating feelings of regret could lead to physical effects such as headaches, sleep problems, high blood pressure, stomach ulcers, and poorly functioning endocrine and immune systems.

If you are indulging in romantic regret, you may undervalue your relationships with friends and family. This could mean that instead of recognising and appreciating the love and support you still have in your life, you place all your energy on that which you lost. You may become swept up in a cycle of self-blame and subsequent self-punishment that could lead to isolating yourself from others. Your loved ones might feel unnecessary strain on their relationships with you. They may feel undervalued or helpless.

"Every day we have plenty of opportunities to get angry, stressed or offended. But what you're doing when you indulge these negative emotions is giving something outside yourself power over your happiness. You can choose to not let little things upset you."
Joel Osteen

Regret can cause you to become fruitlessly obsessed with how your behaviour caused a bad outcome and how you could've done things differently to have avoided said outcome. These thoughts and beliefs may extend for months or even years, causing you long lasting emotional suffering as well as difficulties in every avenue of your life. The following list illustrates some ways your cycling thoughts of regret may be disrupting your everyday life.

Unhelpful Rumination

Cycles of rumination begin with a situation which had a poor or undesirable outcome. They then lead to negative thoughts focused on what you did to cause this outcome. These thoughts lead to negative self-beliefs which are often catastrophic in tone. Subsequently you develop self-limiting or self-sabotaging actions. These patterns may lead to a lifetime of unhappiness or missed opportunities.

Example Situation: The end of a relationship

Thoughts
- I should've paid more attention to…
- I should / shouldn't have said / texted / emailed…
- I should've been more…
- If only I had just…
- I shouldn't have acted so…
- I should've appreciated them more.

Beliefs
- Things could've been different if I…
- They would've loved me more if I…
- This person is the only one for me.
- I pushed them away.
- I am ugly / stupid / useless.
- I am unlovable.
- I don't deserve love.
- I will never have love.
- I will never be happy.
- I am the type of person who cannot be in a relationship.
- I am "bad" at relationships.
- I am "different" from other people.
- I am a bad person.

- Other people deserve better than me.

Actions
- Isolating yourself or becoming socially withdrawn
- Self sabotage in work, future relationships, or home life
- Giving up on the idea of a healthy relationship entirely
- Indulging in casual, meaningless sex
- Excess drinking or drug taking
- Spending excess amounts of money
- Self harm

Example Situation: Loss of a job or financial wealth

Thoughts
- I should've been smarter with my money.
- I should've acted in a different manner.
- I should've thought before I…
- I shouldn't have…

Beliefs
- I deserved what happened to me.
- I am stupid / useless.
- I may never be employed again.
- I will never have that much money again unless…
- I will never achieve success.
- I will be nothing until I…
- I do not deserve happiness.
- I will never be happy.
- I will not deserve any form of happiness until I undo this.
- I do not deserve respect or admiration from others.

Actions
- Becoming isolated or withdrawn
- Self sabotaging relationships or home life
- Ending friendships with people you once worked with due to embarrassment / shame
- Becoming lazy or hyperactive
- Excess drinking or drug taking

- Spending excess amounts of money
- Ending relationships wherein you are happy because of harmful self-beliefs
- Pushing people away or disallowing others to get close to you
- Creating unnecessary limitations on yourself such as "I will not allow myself to rest / love / enjoy anything until I reach a certain financial goal."
- Limiting purchases, vacations, or other luxuries even if you don't have to
- Becoming a "work-a-holic"
- Self harm

Situation: Death of a loved one

Thoughts
- I should've said "I love you" more often.
- I should've said sorry for…
- I should've been a better partner / child / sibling / friend.
- I should've been more agreeable.
- I should've been more understanding.
- I should've asked more questions / been a better listener.
- I should've visited more often.

Beliefs
- I made life hard for this person.
- I could've made things easier.
- I could've prevented this death.
- I am a bad person.
- I am not worthy of love or affection.
- I cause bad things to happen to other people.
- I cause others pain.
- I effect people negatively.
- I should not be around other people.

Actions
- Becoming isolated or withdrawn from others
- Becoming overly affectionate towards / worried about

others
- Becoming obsessed with death or illness
- Ending relationships because of harmful self-beliefs
- Pushing people away or disallowing others to get close to you
- Limiting your possibility for love or happiness
- Excess drinking or drug taking
- Spending excess amounts of money
- Self harm

As you can see, regret can eat you up inside and may cause endless cycles of harmful behaviour. If your life is full of regret, it may lead you to catastrophic beliefs about yourself. If you've had a series of bad relationships, you may believe that you are incapable of having a successful one. This could lead to feelings of being "different" than others which may make you feel deeply unhappy, lost, helpless, or hopeless. Furthermore, your actions will reflect these feelings. You will avoid relationships, act flippant toward others, keep your guard up, and avoid opportunities for potentially successful relationships in the future which will lead you into even more regret.

These kinds of cycles can and will go on forever unless you decide to stop them in their tracks. If you are living a life of regret and avoidance, you must realise that life is better than you are allowing it to be. You must be prepared to try something again. You must be prepared to let go of your past regret and get your head in the game of the present.

"Let today be the day you stop being haunted by the ghost of yesterday. Holding a grudge & harboring anger/resentment is poison to the soul. Get even with people...but not those who have hurt us, forget them, instead get even with those who have helped us."
Steve Maraboli
Life, The Truth and Being Free

The final section of this book is going to show you how to address your feelings of regret, let go of them, and move on from them in order to live a happy and healthy life! But first, here is a quick recap of what you have learned about regret so far.

1.) Regret is based in a belief that you are at fault for a bad outcome in the past. It can make life helpless, hopeless, and unbearable.

2.) The world around you can cause feelings of regret. Advertisements and other people's lives could make you judge yourself harshly and may lead to feelings of regret about your life decisions.

3.) Romantic regret is among the top regrets felt by both sexes.

4.) Though regret in the short term is often felt due to actions taken, in the long term, regret is often more focused on actions not taken and opportunities missed. When interviewed, older people had strong regrets about "playing it safe" and wished they had taken more risks in life.

5.) Regret can cause cycles of limiting self beliefs and life experiences. The more one experiences regret, the more they are likely to avoid taking chances in the future.

Letting Go Of Regret: Live Your Life!

So far you have seen how regret can cause painful rumination and self doubt and you have seen how it can inform the choices you make and the chances you take. You understand that regret is a feeling based in the past and that it is harmful and limiting by nature. You should know now that regret only serves to make you feel bad about yourself and your decisions. You know that regret can hold you back from your potential success and happiness.

This section is going to show you how, in just 5 easy steps, you can free yourself from regret once and for all! Following these 5 steps you will find a short section focusing specifically on romantic regret.

Step One: Identify The What And Why

As with all personal growth, you must understand how regret affects you and your life before you can rid yourself of it for good. This means understanding what you regret and why. It also means understanding what things you are avoiding in the present and how these decisions are based in mistakes and regrets from the past.

Use the following questions to help guide you on a short journey of self understanding so you can better understand how regret is functioning in your life. In order to get the most out of this process, be entirely honest with yourself, this is absolutely vital. That might mean facing up to some painful things about yourself, your decisions, and your past; however, this is a necessary step in self acceptance and ultimate personal freedom.

1.) What do you consciously regret? Write down anything you already admit regretting.

2.) What are you avoiding in life? Write down anything you are holding yourself back from. Think about every avenue in life: love, family, education, career, personal progression, friendships, travelling, socializing, relaxing, and any other thing specific in your life such as learning to drive, following your creative dreams, starting your own business, etc.

3.) Why are you avoiding these things? Take plenty of time with this question. Write down your answers and after you have done so, challenge yourself to dig deeper. If you initially wrote down that you are avoiding relationships because you're "not good at them", go deeper, i.e. because you haven't had a successful relationship yet, because you're afraid of rejection? because you are afraid of trying again, because you might make a mistake or fail, etc.

4.) What self beliefs do you possess that may be informing the limitations you've placed on your life? This may be a painful part of self exploration but it is important to address what beliefs you have of yourself that are holding you back. Are you avoiding a certain path of education because you believe you're a bad learner, unintelligent, or incompetent? Are you avoiding relationships because you believe you are unlovable, unworthy of love, not successful enough, a bad person, etc?

5.) What regret or experience in your past is contributing to your avoidance? Use this question to pinpoint how regret is functioning in your life. Are you avoiding education because you regret doing badly at it in the past? Are you avoiding love because you regret how you handled it in the past? Are you avoiding progression in your career because you regret not doing it when you were younger? Are you avoiding visiting an old friend or relative because you regret how you treated them in the past?

6.) Are avoidance and regret making you feel better or worse? This is the time to ask yourself honestly if your avoidance is making you feel better about yourself. Do you believe that holding yourself back from taking risks is a good thing? Or do you recognise that your limitations merely a mask covering a fear or failure or lack of self confidence that may be rooted in regret from your past? Are you happy to sit with your regret or are you ready to confront it and let it go?

Step Two: Stop The Blame Game!

When it comes to regret, there is no greater enemy than yourself. As you learned earlier, regret isn't just about wishing something had ended differently. It's about blaming yourself for the outcome. It's important to know when it's time to stop the blame game. Blaming yourself isn't just living in the past. It's living in a past where you are in the wrong. Believing that everything is your fault and being overly hard on yourself will only lead to further unhappiness and self loathing. Use the following insight to undo the blame you've placed on yourself.

1.) Be objective.

Instead of looking at yourself as a villain, look at the things you regret from the outside. Take into account all the facts and figures. Think of all the people involved and all the potential outcomes. Think about any contributing circumstances that might've swayed the situation or decision. Ask yourself if what happened was entirely about you or if it was more complicated than that.

2.) Recognise other people's responsibility.

Think about other people's involvement with your regretful situation. Was this thing all about you or were there other people involved? Did everyone else act perfectly and do everything they were supposed to do? Did everyone offer the help or support they could've? Or did others fall short in their responsibilities? Did others place too much pressure on you or bail out when things became difficult? Did someone else let you down or have a bad effect on the situation at hand?

3.) Be realistic.

Look at all the facts and make an honest evaluation of the situation.

Think about how the circumstances surrounding you informed your decisions or actions. Were you too young or inexperienced to know any better at the time? Did you have a limited understanding of the consequences? Were you under a lot of stress or pressure at the time? Were there certain things that were out of your control at the time such as timing, location, or outside influences?

4.) Accept your mistake and let it go.

Hopefully the last three steps helped you realise that you were not solely to blame for what went wrong; however, even if the blame is truly yours and yours alone, is regretting it making any difference to what happened? Regret cannot change a thing about the past. It can only affect how you view yourself now and how you go forward from here. If regret is making you feel bad about yourself it's time to let go. If regret is holding you back from taking risks or getting close to people, it's time to let go. If you did something bad in the past but you feel bad about it now, it is time to accept your wrongdoing, forgive yourself, and move forward now.

Step Three: Letting Go Of "Coulda, Woulda, Shoulda"

There's a lot of wishing in regretting. You wish you had done things differently. You let yourself dwell on how things COULD'VE went, WOULD'VE went, and SHOULD'VE went. You picture yourself reliving the situation but doing everything differently and in your fantasy everything is just perfect. Everyone is happy. No one gets hurt and everything has a fairy tale ending.

However, thoughts like these are not helpful at all. They only reiterate negative feelings about yourself. You have to recognise that regret is keeping you anchored in a past that you cannot change. Regret is keeping anchored in a time you cannot relive and hence, it is holding you back from attention, emotions, and energy required in the present. The longer you spend dwelling on the past the more likely you are to become isolated and depressed.

You must find a way to forgive yourself for your shortcomings and you must let go of all the things you wish you did differently. Now is about now. Let then be about then.

Step Four: Turn Your Regret Into Something Positive!

Regret can be a function of survival in that it teaches you how to recognise when you've made a bad decision and leads you toward making better ones. In the short term, regret can be a warning bell when it's time to make a change. Regret can help you recognise when you are on a negative path. It can help you refocus and pursue a better one. Regret might pose you with a very simple decision: go down a path of self destruction and self loathing or strive to be a better version of yourself.

Harness the functional aspects of your regrets and use them positively. If you are struggling with an addiction or other negative pattern in life, set yourself on a path of change and growth. If you have repeatedly hurt others with a certain behavioral pattern, make a resolve to get out of that pattern and start treating people better. If you have a pattern of self destructing your relationships with others, maybe it's time to address why you are doing that and break the habit.

Life is a journey. Everybody makes mistakes and everyone learns some lessons the hard way. Remember that mistakes can be a good way to get to know yourself and your own personal values. It can awaken you to your own vulnerabilities and needs in life. Regret might help you recognise how to better care for yourself and others.

Step Five: Live In The NOW!

"One must simply take the days of their lives as they happen. If you spend time worrying over what is to come, which may or may not happen, then you will only be wasting precious days you will wish in the future you could have cherished a bit longer."
RJ. Gonzales

So far, I have talked extensively about forgiving yourself for past mistakes. However, let us not forget that statistics show that older individuals regret things that *didn't* do more than things they *did* do. This is such an important thing to remember! Earlier you took some time to look at how regret is causing you to avoid doing certain things in your life. You recognized how regrets about your past are holding you back from taking risks.

You will probably remember what you learned about regret causing cyclical behaviour. To refresh your memory, if you regret something in the past, you'll be worried about taking risks in the present and the future. And if you let those worries hold you back from living a rich and happy life, you will ultimately be full of regret when you reach the end of your journey. This is a harmful and limiting cycle to get caught in. It is a way of living that is based in fear and regret.

"You can clutch the past so tightly to your chest that it leaves your arms too full to embrace the present."
Jan Glidewell

Lives that are rich with experience lead to overall contentment in life. If you want to feel content at the end of your life, you can rest assured that worrying about the future and feeling sorry about the past will not get you there.

Prevent the regret you might feel about lost opportunities by taking risks!

Seize the day!

Stop waiting for the perfect time to start living. **Live life NOW.**

Step Six: Getting To Grips With Romantic Regret

If you are experiencing romantic regret about an experience in your recent or distant past, you might be causing yourself further emotional damage and pain by avoiding relationships entirely, placing limitations or rules on your relationships, or being overly sensitive or guarded with other people.

Being careful with your emotions is healthy and natural. Being selective about who you get close to is smart. However, if you are notice that you have a pattern of holding back, controlling relationships, or ending relationships prematurely, it's time to get to grips with whatever is holding you back. Often after experiencing an unhealthy or unhappy relationship (or multiple relationships), you might stop believing that you could actually have a healthy one. Like any failure, when you have experienced romantic failures, you can lose confidence in your own capability of a romantic success. You might experience disbelief in yourself and may find yourself unworthy of love, affection, and happiness. Feelings like this might make you run away from relationships even when they are going well.

This text is not going to tell you just hang in there if something is actually wrong within your relationship. On the contrary, it seeks to awaken you to certain destructive behaviours you might be exhibiting that are keeping you from allowing others to get close to you.

Human beings are born into groups. We are born into a family and we are designed, like many other animal species, to spend our lives with and around others. Expressions of love, affection, and physical contact have been proven to cure depression and physical illness, boost the immune system, and extend the lifespan of human beings.

In addition, every human being will experience some benefit from receiving respect, understanding, and acceptance from another. For this reason, you could say that loving relationships are an integral part of a full happy life.

If you have had bad experiences with relationships in the past, it's important to remind yourself that failures in the past do not dictate how you can succeed in the present or the future. It is important to recognise that all people are different, and hence, all relationships are different. Not all relationships follow the conventional blueprint and what went wrong with one relationship will not necessarily go wrong in another. Believing that you cannot have a healthy relationship might cause to you pushing people away and end up later feeling bitter, resentful, alienated, and lonely.

If you are the type of person who refuses to let love into your life because you are afraid you might fail at it, it is time to let go of the regret keeping you anchored in the past. Remember again, the survey that showed how older individuals regretted most the risks they did not take. You cannot predict the future any more than you can change the past. There is a fine line between protecting yourself and limiting your life on earth. If you know deep down that you make excuses to keep yourself from being loved ask yourself why. If you think no one could love you because of your past, you are wrong. If you think no one could love you because of your lifestyle, you're wrong. If you think someone might get to know the "real you" and later reject you, you're trying to predict the future. By running away from risks you are limiting yourself and letting your past regrets determine your present and your future.

Let go of limitations and live in the now! If you feel strongly about someone, don't hold back. If you fail, you fail. But if you succeed, you succeed!

6 Steps To A Positive Life

Step 1: Believe Happiness is a Choice
For me, this was a hard one at first. I thought that people were either unhappy or happy (and I was one of the unhappy ones). I used to blame this on all kinds of outside forces -- fate, experiences, parents, relationships -- but never really stopped to think that I could *choose* to be happy.
Sure, this isn't always easy, but it is always, always an option. Teaching myself to see that happiness is a choice has been one of the greatest things I've ever done for myself.
Now when I find myself in a bad situation, I know that it's up to me to find the good, to be happy regardless of what's happening around me. I am no longer pointing fingers, placing blame. I realize that everything happens how it happens and it's up to me to choose how I want to feel about it. I am in control of my happiness level and no one can take that away from me.

Step 2: Rid Your Life of Negativity
If you want to live a positive, joyful and happy life, you cannot -- absolutely CANNOT -- be surrounded by negative people who are not encouraging your happiness. When I was a pretty negative person, I tended to attract other negative people.
When I decided to make the change to live a more positive life, I had to rid my life of all of the negative people in it. This, as you can imagine, wasn't easy. Getting rid of people hurts -- even when you know they aren't good for you or your current lifestyle.
Not only did I have to get rid of the negative people, but I also had to get rid of the negative things too. I had to stop doing certain things that were causing negativity in my life. I had to take a step back and examine which behaviors were good for me and which were not.
I learned to focus on the positive things I was doing and let go of the negative ones. This process was not easy and to be honest, is still ongoing, but I know this: having negativity in your life prevents you from living a truly positive existence.

Step 3: Look For the Positive in Life
There is the positive aspect in everything. In every person, in every

situation, there is something good. Most of the time it's not all that obvious. We have to look. And sometimes we have to look hard. The old me just sat back and allowed things to happen by default. If I saw negative, I went with that feeling. I didn't want to look harder or think too much about the good. I found it much, much easier to sit back and just accept what I saw (which was usually the bad).
Now, when I'm faced with a difficult or challenging situation, I think to myself, *"What is good about this?"* No matter how terrible the situation might seem, I always can find something good if I take the time to think about it.
Everything — good and bad — is a learning experience. So, at the very least, you can learn from bad experiences. However, there's usually even more to it than that. If you really take the time to look, you will usually find something good, something really positive, about every person or situation.

Step 4: Reinforce Positivity in Yourself
Once I started thinking more positively and adapted to a more positive attitude, I realized I had to reinforce these thoughts and behaviors in myself so they would stick. As with any sort of training, practice makes perfect, and, yes, you can practice being positive.
The best and easiest way to do this is to be positive when it comes to who you are. Tell yourself you're awesome. Tell yourself you look good. Tell yourself that you **love and accept yourself** completely. Tell yourself you did an awesome job at work or raising your kids or whatever it is you do.
Be honest with yourself, but do your best to look for the good. And, whatever you do, *don't* focus on the negative. Nothing good can come of telling yourself that your butt's too big or your latest career goal wasn't met.
It's okay to not like everything about yourself (yet), but don't spend energy dwelling on the negative. Remind yourself of the good in you. We all have positive attributes and it's up to you to remind yourself of them every day.

Step 5: Share Happiness with Others
Not only do you need to be positive with yourself for this new *positive attitude* to really take effect, you also need to be positive with others. You have to share your wealth of positivity with the

world.

The best way I've found to do this is quite simple and basic: be nice. Be nice to other people, no matter what. Tell someone he or she looks nice today. Tell someone they did a great job on that presentation. Tell your parents or children (or both!) how much you love them and how great they are.

When someone is feeling down, do what you can to cheer him or her up. Send flowers. Write notes. Don't gossip. Be kind to all living things. All of these things sound basic enough, but, for someone like me, they didn't used to come easily.

In the past, I didn't wanted to see the good in myself and, therefore, didn't want to see it in others either. I used to be critical and condescending. Now I strive to be encouraging and supportive. I try not only to treat others, as I would like to be treated, but also to consider how *they* would like to be treated.

People appreciate positivity and the more you are sharing it with others, the more you are practicing it and reinforcing it in your own life.

Step 6: Be The Owner Of Your Life

As author Kate Anderson said in her best selling book "100 Positive Morning Thoughts" (Highly recommended!):

"Though we must be good to one another and value the needs and beliefs of others, we must also remember that each of our lives is important, including yours! If you are the type of person who puts other people first at all costs, it's time to turn the focus on yourself. Caring for and helping others in your life is good, but if you're not careful, you may lose yourself along the way. Similarly, if you allow others to make decisions in your life or bully you into living a way you don't agree with, you will find yourself resentful and unhappy. Stand up for who you are and vow to get what you want out of life. Prioritize yourself and your needs. Know when to say "no". Own your life."

Start Living Today!

In this text, I have shown you how worry, embarrassment, and regret can have detrimental effects on your happiness, your relationships with others, your self beliefs, and your true potential. This is centered around the belief that these three self conscious emotions anchor your thoughts in the past and the future; thus, keeping you from fully living in the present.

Spending your life worrying about the future will not prevent bad things from happening, it will only prevent you from enjoying life in the present and hold you back from future progression. Let me repeat that: spending your life worrying about the future will NOT prevent bad things from happening.

Allowing embarrassment to rule over you is no more than being your own bully. Reliving embarrassing moments serves no purpose other than to make you feel bad about yourself. Comparing yourself to others is not useful in your life. In order to be happy with yourself and your decisions, you must judge yourself by your own standards and your own criteria. Feelings of shame and regret will get in the way of self-love, and good self-care.

Letting go of worry, embarrassment, and regret will allow you to let go of the unpredictable future and the unchangeable past so that you can enjoy the ever changing and ever exciting present.

Live today. Be healthy and happy. This is your life.

jenniferalisonauthor.com

Subscribe to the Dr. Jennifer Alison mailing list for news of new releases, free eBooks and exclusive extra content.

Sign up by clicking here and receive a FREE book of tips to

deal with anxiety fast: http://eepurl.com/bwU1Rv

Other Books Available By Jennifer Alison

Overcome Social Anxiety In The Workplace In One Week
Panic Attacks & Anxiety

Recommended Books

The following list of books come highly recommended. I have hand picked only the works that have actively helped my clients and my colleagues clients.

100 Positive Morning Thoughts by Kate Anderson

100 Positive Ideas & Thoughts by Kate Anderson

Rising Strong by Brene Brown

21 Days To Master Success & Inner Peace by Dr Wayne W. Dyer

The 7 Habits Of Highly Effective People by Stephen R. Covey

Printed in Great Britain
by Amazon